Played in Manchester

The architectural heritage of a city at play

Played in Manchester
© English Heritage 2004

English Heritage
is the government's statutory
advisor on all aspects of the
historic environment

23 Savile Row
London W1X 1AB
www.english-heritage.org.uk

Design by Doug Cheeseman

Additional research by
Clare Hartwell & Jason Wood
Maps by Mark Fenton
For image credits see page 134

Malavan Media is a creative
consultancy responsible
for the Played in Britain series
www.playedinbritain.co.uk

Printed by Zrinski, Croatia
ISBN: 1 87359 2787
Product Code: 50945

Played in Manchester

The architectural heritage of a city at play

Simon Inglis

ENGLISH HERITAGE

MANCHESTER
CITY COUNCIL

Withington Baths, Burton Road (*right*), opened its doors in 1913 and retains many original features, including its coloured glass panels, floor tiling and Salford-made Ellison's turnstiles. Designed by the City of Manchester's Architects Department under the directorship of Henry Price, Withington is the oldest functioning public baths in the Manchester area. Its interior is shown on page 122.

Page Two The Northern Lawn Tennis Club, Palatine Road, Didsbury, stages its annual Northern Tournament – the Wimbledon of the North – in the early 1950s. Around 700 spectators are accommodated on temporary seats around two show courts. The club's mock-Tudor pavilion (*seen top left*) was originally erected in 1881 at the Northern's first grounds in Old Trafford, where Tennis Street is now located (*see back cover*).

Page One The delightful former Manchester Grammar School pavilion at the Lower Broughton Playing Fields, Salford, was designed by James Murgatroyd of Mills and Murgatroyd and opened by the Lord Mayor of Manchester on August 1 1899. It cost £1,125 to build, plus £782 to drain and prepare the pitches. Remarkably intact over a century later, the pavilion is still in use by local schools.

Contents

Foreword

by Councillor Richard Leese, Leader of Manchester City Council

Among the many happy sporting memories I shall always cherish, Aisha Hansen's last gasp victory in the 2002 Commonwealth Games triple jump has to be one of the best.

For ten magical days that summer, while Hansen and her fellow athletes from around the Commonwealth thrilled us all, Manchester showed the world what a great city it is, and how passionate we are about sport. Not just about our two great football clubs, City and United, but about all sports; from athletics and bowls to wrestling and weightlifting.

With over 900,000 tickets sold at the 38 venues, Manchester did itself, and Britain proud. By common consent, ours was the best Commonwealth Games ever.

Nor should we forget our efforts in staging Euro 96 and our hosting of the UEFA Champions League final in 2003. Or the fact that in parallel with the 2002 Games the city organised the successful Spirit of Friendship cultural festival, a Commonwealth Film Festival and the memorable Queen's Jubilee

Baton Relay, which took the Commonwealth Games message to 500 locations around the UK.

At least 24,000 local people volunteered for involvement in these and other 2002 activities, and I doubt if any will ever forget the experiences they shared.

This book is the direct result of another Games related initiative.

We at the City Council were delighted when, a few months before the Games, we learnt that English Heritage had chosen Manchester as the focus for the country's first ever detailed study of sporting heritage.

Our city's built heritage is already known and admired throughout the architectural world. We also can claim some of urban Britain's most celebrated landscapes, such as Philips Park, one of the first municipal parks in Britain, opened in 1846, and the sweeping Irwell Valley.

But what is perhaps less appreciated, even by those of us who know the city well, is the strength and depth of our sporting heritage. The Victoria Baths are now justifiably famous, thanks to

the BBC *Restoration* programme. But how many more fine and historic sporting gems we have.

Manchester, we now learn, played a crucial role in the early development of ice rinks. We have three of the oldest functioning Lads' Clubs in Britain. The Moor Lane sports ground, it turns out, has been in continuous use for sporting activity for over 300 years.

I was also intrigued to discover that Salford supplied turnstiles to the world for most of the 20th century, and that Belle Vue witnessed the birth of modern greyhound racing in Britain.

English Heritage's researchers discovered so much of interest in their pilot study that they decided to turn their findings into this book and to make Manchester the launchpad for the *Played in Britain* series as a whole.

With so many sporting firsts under our belt we are glad they did, and in sponsoring this fascinating publication, hope that *Played in Manchester* will bring added interest to all those who live here, or who come as visitors to this great city that we love so much.

Colin Spofforth's inspiring bronze sculpture – The Runner – displayed outside the Manchester Regional Arena at Sportcity, expresses the power, beauty and sense of liberation that sport engenders.

◄ *Top left* A personalised crown green bowl, made from lignum vitae (a now protected form of hardwood), awaiting restoration by Premier Bowls of Stockport.
Below left A medicine ball found at the Salford Lads' Club, Ordsall, possibly supplied when the club opened in 1904.

Top right The 1948 FA Cup Final ball used when Manchester United beat Blackpool 4-2, on display at the Manchester United museum.
Below right Another vintage lignum vitae bowl, c.1880, from the skittle alley of the Manchester Tennis and Racquet Club, on Blackfriars Road, Salford.

Introduction

by Malcolm Cooper, English Heritage

This detail from an undated painting in the Lancashire County Cricket Club museum at Old Trafford appears to be from the period when cricket first established itself in the Manchester and Salford areas, between 1815-25. An early set of rules belonging to Broughton Cricket Club, formed in 1823, states that no fielder be permitted to smoke or lie down during play.

As many of us who live and work in this great city of Manchester are surely aware, sport plays a fundamental role in the health and welfare of our communities. Whether one plays or watches, swims or runs, kicks or catches; whether one is for the Reds or the Blues, the Sharks or the Aces, or even if one is only dimly aware of crowds gathering, of games being played, of hopes being raised or dashed, we can hardly fail to recognise that sport is as much a part of the fabric of city life as are the arts, the sciences, commerce and industry.

As the public body responsible for protecting and promoting the historic environment, English Heritage has, over the years, undertaken the study of a diverse range of building types. Our work with ancient monuments, churches, great houses and buildings at risk is well known.

But in addition to conservation, another part of our role is to address our fieldwork and analysis to specific building types, or sites, that are poorly understood, and which may be at risk as a result.

We have in recent years, for example, made great advances in our understanding of industrial structures (factories, mills and so on), domestic architecture (such as back-to-back housing and prefabs), commercial and leisure-oriented buildings (shops, cinemas and public houses) and even telephone and post boxes.

We also maintain a register of historic parks and gardens, which now includes some 1500 sites, amongst them a number of public parks in the Manchester area.

Given these areas of concern, we are delighted therefore to turn to the subject of sport, and in particular to this brand new series of English Heritage publications under the inspirational title of *Played in Britain*.

Starting with *Played in Manchester* we hope the series will develop into a wide ranging, comprehensive and informative record of the best of this nation's extraordinarily rich sporting heritage.

And it is quite extraordinary.

Incredibly, most of the sports played at international level today – including football (by far the world's most popular sport), cricket, rugby (both union and league), hockey, tennis (both lawn and real), bowls (both crown green and flat green), golf, archery, water polo, snooker... the list goes on – were either invented, or at the very least developed, honed and codified for popular consumption by British sportsmen and women, administrators and officials.

But what of British sport's architectural heritage?

Sports architecture, and the very places where sport is played – the parks and gardens of sport, as it were – have not enjoyed the level of attention that many people feel they deserve and need.

As a result, a number of buildings and sites have been lost before their historic, architectural and social worth has been properly assessed.

This rate of loss has been especially accelerated in the last decade or so following the much stricter health and safety guidelines imposed since the terrible tragedies at Bradford in 1985 and Hillsborough in 1989.

Sport's more rigorous safety regime has placed considerable pressure on our older facilities.

Yet it has also led to the creation of some of the wonderful new facilities we see all around, not least in the north west, where the 2002 Commonwealth Games has helped transform the cityscape with a number of breathtaking venues; the City of Manchester Stadium at Sportcity, for example.

In turning our attention to sporting heritage we are therefore not turning our backs on progress.

On the contrary, because the pace of modernisation is so rapid, now is the absolutely the right time to take stock of what historic buildings and sites we have, and make sure that we evaluate them, record them, and where appropriate, work with partners to ensure that they are either conserved for sporting use, or adapted for other uses that will secure their long term viability.

It was to assist us in this process that in 2001 English Heritage's North West Region decided to commission a pilot study entitled *A Sporting Chance - Extra Time for England's Historic Sports Venues*.

Furthermore, with the Commonwealth Games on the horizon, we decided to focus specifically on Manchester.

Starting with a blank sheet of paper and no preconceptions, project leader and heritage consultant, Jason Wood, and his team of experts (Simon Inglis, Clare Hartwell, Julie Graham, Gill Chitty and Frank Kelsall) took on the not inconsiderable task of mapping out the issues that might inform English Heritage's future approach to sporting heritage at a national level.

As they soon established, this is a complex, often emotionally charged area in which there are scores of examples of interesting buildings, highly cherished by their owners and users, but many others where disuse and dereliction has set in.

Not surprisingly they found that one man's shrine is often another man's unwanted eyesore.

Conversely, they also came across apparently humble buildings or sites which turned out to be far more significant than even regular users were aware.

Here are just a few of the examples featured in this book.

Manchester, the study was able to establish, has the three oldest purpose-built Lads' Clubs still in active use in Britain today, one of which, the Salford Lads' Club, has recently been listed Grade II.

Probably the oldest sports ground in Manchester, it transpires, is on Moor Lane, which we now know formed part of Manchester's first proper racecourse at Kersal Moor in 1681, and has been open space set aside for sport ever since. Behind the ground is a road, Nevile Road, whose route follows almost exactly the path of the racecourse itself.

We discovered why there is a Tennis Street in Old Trafford, a Cricket Street in Denton, and a Robin Hood pub in Cheetham Hill. We found a delightful 1960s turnstile block at the Belle Vue greyhound stadium, which is also, incidentally, the oldest greyhound stadium in Britain; a well preserved Edwardian billiard room in an Eccles pub; a modernist bowls and tennis pavilion in Wythenshawe Park, and a Salford company which is only one of two left in the world making wooden lacrosse sticks. We found an historic real tennis club within a short stroll of the city centre which

even some of the city's sporting cognoscenti did not know existed.

We learnt that the now empty Manchester Ice Palace in Derby Street, built in 1910, is the oldest surviving rink in Britain, but that one of the first ice rinks in the world had been in Rusholme.

And of course we were all reminded of the deep emotional ties that bind people to buildings when the disused Victoria Baths in Hathersage Road attracted an avalanche of votes to win BBC Television's *Restoration* series in 2003, an initative that English Heritage was happy to support.

Played in Manchester represents just one aspect of the work carried in the pilot study; the site visits and the related historical research.

Another vital element of the study was a comprehensive survey of public views and attitudes.

Jason Wood and his colleagues talked to hundreds of individuals; officials of governing bodies, representatives of strategic authorities, local planners, club officials and historians, sports fans and players. They asked, what do Mancunians think about sporting heritage? 》

As the groundsman's sign at Manchester United's Old Trafford stadium suggests, visitors from overseas love to visit Britain's many famous sports venues. United's museum, which opened in 1998, attracts up to 250,000 visitors a year and is one of the north west's leading tourist attractions. Manchester City now have their own museum too, at the City of Manchester Stadium. But might other sports-related sites in the Manchester area also be of interest, to local residents as well as to visitors and tourists? Could a greater understanding of sporting heritage help to regenerate certain areas of the city, or help revive pride in neglected grounds and open urban spaces?

Sports clubs not only fulfil an important role in promoting health and community life. They also act as the unofficial guardians of a substantial proportion of our urban green space. Stamford Bowling Club in the centre of Altrincham (*above*), play on a green that dates back to at least 1844 and is part of a Conservation Area. Even non-bowlers recognise the importance of this historic open space. But in October 2004 the club faced eviction after a massive rent rise, and the future of the green is now in serious doubt. Hundreds of bowls and other urban sports clubs have succumbed to pressure from developers in recent decades.

》 Which buildings and which sports-related sites did they believe were of interest, or of importance?

And what criteria did they use in making those assessments?

Were these buildings and locations valued for their architectural qualities, or for their cultural significance, for their associations with specific individuals, or events perhaps? Or simply because they were part of the local scene and fitted in well with the surroundings?

When speaking of sporting heritage, as one would expect, respondents often emphasised the value of tradition, and of the sense of belonging and identity that well established sports clubs engender.

Often location was deemed more important than modernity. Nor were new facilities necessarily wanted if costs were likely to rise as a result. Above all, a clear majority emphasised that access to affordable and accessible sports facilities and open spaces was the most important factor in their judgement, and that these amenities needed protection.

But it also became clear that there are no hard and fast rules. Every case has to be judged on its merits, while everyone seemed to agree that the needs of spectators and players should not come second to that of conservation.

Many hard working club officials spoke a great deal about both the pleasures and pains they experience in looking after much loved but creaking properties; of the costs of basic maintenance and of the difficult balance they face between preserving the best of what they have – because this was part of their club's appeal – while at the same time needing to offer more modern facilities in order to attract younger members.

Many in this position felt strongly that they were not given enough help or support to preserve their buildings and open spaces. All the advice they were getting from governing bodies and funding agencies was geared towards replacement rather than renewal.

Two reports which readers may find offer a useful background to the *Played in Britain* series are *Power of Place: the Future of the Historic Environment* (English Heritage, 2000) and *The Historic Environment: A Force for Our Future* (DCMS 2001). Both are listed in the Links section on page 130.

Both documents emphasise the need to widen public access to the historic environment, to take into account those aspects of the historic environment that people value most, and to engage those people who feel excluded from the planning process.

All these and a number of other recommendations relating to the future management of our historic environment apply equally to sport.

For some groups within society, indeed, sport clearly offers an ideal platform on which to build a greater awareness and appreciation of our wider heritage.

Inevitably this book is only a small step in a much longer process. Many of the issues highlighted by the study go far beyond the remit of English Heritage.

Also inevitably the approach we have taken will not meet with universal approval.

For example, it might seem odd to readers that we have not dedicated individual chapters to major sports such as football and cricket, whereas there are sections on minority sports such as archery and lacrosse.

This was deliberate, partly because we felt that the historical background to those sports is already well covered in other works – of which a select few are listed in the Links section – but also because our emphasis is on areas that we feel are less well known, or researched, and may therefore merit wider recognition.

Equally, there are several sports which, in the Manchester area at least, do not possess or are not associated with any historic buildings or sites. Hockey is one such example.

In other cities, no doubt, other sports would come to the fore, while others that are strong in Manchester, such as lacrosse, might not feature at all.

While calling this book *Played in Manchester* we also fully acknowledge that the study area takes in not only the city of Manchester but also Salford, parts of Trafford, Tameside and Stockport. It does not extend to the Greater Manchester areas of Bolton, Rochdale or Oldham. 》

▲ Rita McBride's **Arena** is one of 35 artworks located on the **Irwell Sculpture Trail**, a Lottery-funded joint venture between the Arts Council of England, Salford City Council and three other local authorities straddling the Irwell.

Five metres tall, the 'sculptural amphitheatre' sits atop a turf embankment overlooking the river, the Littleton Road Playing Fields and Manchester United's Academy Ground (*see map on page 35*).

Speaking at its installation in 2002, McBride explained, 'I have always been fascinated by the structures and the scale of structures built for spectacle.'

It is a fascination shared by many, drawn not only towards the action, but towards the intimacy of enclosed spaces and the hum of the crowd. No-one who watches or plays sport needs to be persuaded of the power of place, or of the value of historic sporting locations.

Indeed based on the idea of a sculpture trail, an Irwell Valley sports heritage trail – and a similar one in Old Trafford perhaps – might be one practical way to celebrate this important part of our shared cultural and historic legacy.

» Limited by time and resources, we chose as our boundaries the area lying within the M60 motorway belt, with occasional forays beyond – to the likes of Davyhulme, Ashton, Altrincham and Stockport – only in cases where we considered there to be buildings of specific interest or relevance to the overall story of sporting heritage in the Manchester area.

The map opposite shows the extent of the study area and the key sites featured within the book.

To all those who feel strongly that, as separate political entitities, Salford, Trafford, Tameside and Stockport should not be bracketed within the general heading of Manchester, or that entries from Radcliffe or Oldham should have taken precedence over ones from Sale or Urmston, we offer our sincerest apologies.

But to borrow a sporting phrase, the referee's decision is final. We had to draw a line somewhere.

One last caveat. It is not this book's aim to express English Heritage's policy.

Nor does it set out to tell the story of sport in Manchester.

Rather, it offers a guide to the city's history, as told through its sports buildings.

This is, admittedly, a novel approach, and one we recognise may well prompt discussion. But

that is only to be welcomed. As stated earlier, this is the first step on a long journey.

We nevertheless hope that it will help to inform and delight all those whose lives are touched by sport, in one way or another.

We wish to thank Manchester City Council for their generous support for *Played in Manchester*. Their commitment is yet another demonstration of what sport means to the city and its people.

Finally, one of the most rewarding aspects of the Manchester study has been the goodwill and support we received from across the city's sporting fraternity – a testament not only to people's desire to celebrate our sporting heritage, but also, we feel, to the positive character of the many individuals in this city who dedicate much of their lives, often without financial reward, to the sustenance of community life.

We hope that *Played in Manchester* will help to make those people's efforts more appreciated, and supported.

We also hope that readers will be spurred into visiting and enjoying the many fascinating sites featured in the book, and in the process, help to ensure that this city's wonderful sporting heritage will be recognised, celebrated and safeguarded for many years to come.

Map References

1. **Ellesmere Sports Club**, Walkden Road (*72*)
2. **Barton Aerodrome**, Liverpool Road (*115*)
3. **Davyhulme Park Golf Course** (*75*)
4. **Stamford Bowls Club**, Church Walk, Altrincham (*10/83*)
5. **Sale Football Club**, Heywood Road (*61*)
6. **Wythenshawe Park bowls & tennis club** (*84*)
7. **Grange Bowls Club**, Edgeley Road, Stockport (*85*)
8. **Stockport Cricket, Bowls and Lacrosse Club**, Cale Green (*91-92*)
9. **Stockport Lads' Club**, Hempshaw Lane (*109*)
10. **Henry Square Baths**, Ashton-under-Lyne (*119*)
11. **St Leonard's Church**, Middleton (*77*)
12. **Heaton Park Bowling Facility**, St Margaret's Road (*84*)
13. **Harpurhey Baths**, Rochdale Road (*120*)
14. **Robin Hood pub** and **St Mark's graveyard** (*79*)
15. former **Hot Shots Snooker Club**, Cheetham Hill (*112*)
16. **Moor Lane sports ground**, Kersal (*37*)
17. former **Castle Irwell racecourse**, Cromwell Road (*38-40*)
18. **The Cliff** / former **MGS Pavilion**, Lower Broughton Road (*43/1*)
19. **Broughton Pool**, Great Cheetham Street West (*127*)
20. **Manchester Ice Palace**, Derby Street (*97-99*)
21. **Manchester Evening News Arena**, Victoria Station (*101*)
22. **Greengate Baths**, Collier Street, Salford (*116-118*)
23. **Manchester Tennis & Racquet Club**, Blackfriars Road (*86-89*)
24. **Salford Lads' and Girls' Club**, St Ignatius Walk, Ordsall (*103-107*)
25. **The Willows**, Salford Reds Rugby League ground (*59/61*)
26. **Worsley Golf Club**, Stableford Avenue, Monton (*73*)
27. **Lamb public house**, Regent Street, Eccles (*110-111*)
28. **Old Trafford football stadium**, Sir Matt Busby Way (*32-33*)
29. **Old Trafford Bowling Club**, Talbot Road (*83*)
30. **Old Trafford cricket ground**, Warwick Road (*30-31*)
31. **Longford Park Stadium**, Longford Park (*63*)
32. **Sedge Lynn pub**, Manchester Road, Chorlton (*112*)
33. **Lloyds Bowls Club**, Wilbraham Road (*82*)
34. **Alexandra Park**, Princess Road (*81/121*)
35. **Hough End**, Princess Road (*115*)
36. **Withington Baths**, Burton Road (*4/122*)
37. **Northern Tennis Club**, Palatine Road (*2/26*)
38. **Paulhan Road**, Burnage (*114*)
39. **Burnage Garden Estate**, Burnage (*71*)
40. **Firs Pavilion**, Moseley Road (*74*)
41. **Belle Vue greyhound stadium**, Kirkmanshulme Lane (*50-51*)
42. **Victoria Baths**, Hathersage Road (*123-125*)
43. **Simon Archery Collection**, Manchester Museum, Oxford Road (*78*)
44. **Aquatics Centre**, Booth Street East (*127*)
45. **Ardwick Lads' Club**, Palmerston Street (*105*)
46. **Crossley House Youth Centre**, Ashton Old Road (*108-109*)
47. **Whitworth Baths**, Ashton Old Road (*120*)
48. **City of Manchester Stadium**, Alan Turing Way (*52-57*)
49. **National Cycling Centre**, Stuart Street (*55*)
50. **Philips Park**, Alan Turing Way (*54/121*)

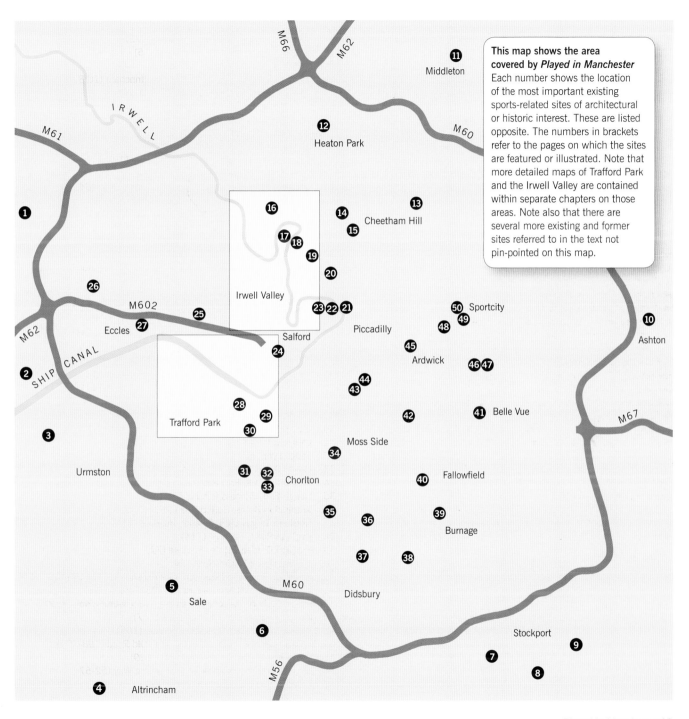

This map shows the area covered by *Played in Manchester* Each number shows the location of the most important existing sports-related sites of architectural or historic interest. These are listed opposite. The numbers in brackets refer to the pages on which the sites are featured or illustrated. Note that more detailed maps of Trafford Park and the Irwell Valley are contained within separate chapters on those areas. Note also that there are several more existing and former sites referred to in the text not pin-pointed on this map.

Middleton

Heaton Park

Cheetham Hill

Irwell Valley

M602

Eccles

Salford

Piccadilly

Sportcity

Ashton

Ardwick

Trafford Park

Belle Vue

Urmston

Moss Side

Chorlton

Fallowfield

Burnage

Sale

Didsbury

Stockport

Altrincham

Chapter One

Played in Manchester

Wrestlers at the Victoria Baths, Hathersage Road, one of six stained glass windows depicting sportsmen, thought to have been crafted by William Pointer of Cundiff and Pointer, London Road, at the time of the baths' construction in 1903-06. Several Manchester Corporation baths of this period featured stained glass. Surviving examples are also at Withington and Harpurhey.

Manchester's contribution to the arts, science, medicine, political thinking and, not least, to commerce and industry, is thoroughly documented and widely acknowledged.

But Manchester has also been extremely active, and influential, in the field of sport.

The following may appear to be a statement of the obvious, but the Manchester area has two international standard football stadiums, a Test and County cricket ground, senior clubs in both rugby league and rugby union, a speedway team, a greyhound stadium, a velodrome, nationally recognised clubs for both lawn tennis and real tennis, the largest indoor arena in Europe, an Olympic size swimming pool, two athletics stadiums, one indoor athletics track, a water sports centre and a hockey centre.

London apart, no other British city offers as diverse a range of facilities at such a high level.

Other than football, cricket and rugby, the Manchester area has, at one time or another, been a leading centre for archery,

Manchester boasts many fine sports venues, but since Castle Irwell closed in 1963 it has had no racecourse, the longest break in a tradition stretching back to the first races on Barlow Moor in 1647. Over 150 years after the last race at Kersal Moor (*right*), which served from 1681-1847, it is still possible to trace the route of the course (*see pp36 and 135*).

athletics, cycling, lacrosse, water polo and speedway.

It is the home of more sports governing bodies than any city outside London. These include the national associations of cycling, lacrosse, squash and wrestling. Also in Manchester are the offices of the Professional Footballers' Association and a branch of the English Institute of Sport.

A city with all these attributes is clearly a city whose people like to play, and that is what this series is all about. Britain at play.

There are many ways of 'reading' a city; getting to grips with its history, its people, its geography, its built environment; its subtle shifts and moods, its character and aspirations.

Played in Manchester seeks to study and reflect all those characteristics through the medium of sport.

More precisely,

our aim is to develop an appreciation of which buildings are of significance, in architectural or in historical terms.

Because this study is part of a wider endeavour, it is also necessary to assess this level of significance against national, and perhaps even international criteria where appropriate.

Similar criteria will equally be applied to the *places* of sport. After all, a sporting landscape, even the humblest patch of green, may be significant with or without any associated structures.

The book is divided into four sections.

This introductory section will briefly outline the development of sport in the Manchester area.

We then go on to study four specific areas; Trafford Park, the Irwell Valley, Belle Vue and Sportcity.

MANCHESTER RACES, 1794.

MONDAY, June the 9th, a Sweep-flakes of Twenty GUINEAS each, With an addition of Fifty Guineas, given to the Subscribers, by the Renters of the Race Ground, for all ages; Mares and Geldings allowed 3lb. Best of 3 four-mile heats.

Earl of Stamford's bay colt, by Wenzle 7ft. 2 blye   fell
John Clifton Efqr's bay horfe, Citizen. 9ft. Peers, brown and yellow   won at 1 beat
John Ford Efqr's chf horfe, Regulus 8ft. 11

These areas have been selected because they contain what may be termed 'clusters' of venues, whose origins, ownership, or patterns of useage may have common roots, or whose development might illustrate common themes.

Most cities have such clusters, and it is usually instructive to find out how and why they came about. Doing so can also provide a range of fresh insights into the character of a city, especially if one is prepared to tour the area on foot.

After the four clusters are chapters on selected stadiums and grounds, clubs and pavilions, in the Manchester area. These are interspersed with a chapter on turnstiles. Since the late 19th century most spectator venues have installed turnstiles, and as it happens, the majority were manufactured in Salford.

The remaining chapters focus on individual sports.

As Malcolm Cooper wrote in his introduction, our choice of sports may seem somewhat eccentric. However, each one is selected first and foremost for the quality and interest of its architectural legacy.

In addition to architecture are the three further 'A's that combine to form the secondary thrust of *Played in Britain's* research agenda: namely the art, artefacts and archaeology of sporting heritage.

Pre-Victorian sport

Here is the programme for the Eccles Wake week, some time in the late 18th century.

'On Monday morning at eleven o'clock the sports will commence with that most ancient, loyal, rational, constitutional and lawful diversion, bull baiting, in all its primitive excellence; for which this place has long been noted.

'At one o'clock there will be a foot race; at two o'clock a bull baiting, for a horse's collar; at four, donkey races for a pair of panniers; at five, a race for a stuff hat; the day's sport to conclude with baiting the bull "Fury" for a superior dog chain.'

On the following days there was to be 'a smock race by ladies'.

There is a common view that sport as we know it today is essentially a Victorian construct.

This is not wholly accurate. But it is the case that before the 19th century the term 'sport' generally referred to bloodsports, such as bear baiting, hunting, hawking or cock-fighting, and also to any form of gambling.

Bull and bear baitings were enjoyed by all classes of society. Queen Elizabeth particularly enjoyed them. But they had their opponents too. A reporter from the *Manchester Gazette*, writing of a baiting at Eccles in 1800, described the event as consisting of 'four and two legged brutes – asses in various shapes…'

'Cursing and swearing and drinking and gambling were natural concomitants of such a brutal pastime…' wrote another observer, this time of a bull baiting at the Jolly Butcher Inn, Alkrington.

'The yelling and shouting of the onlookers was something fearful,' while the promoters (usually butchers who claimed that baiting made the creature's flesh taste better) 'seemed glutted with savage delight.'

Baitings commonly concluded with heavy drinking and fights amid the piles of dead and dying dogs left rotting in the streets.

Another popular venue for bull baiting was Chorlton Green, where the publicans of the Bowling Green Hotel and the »

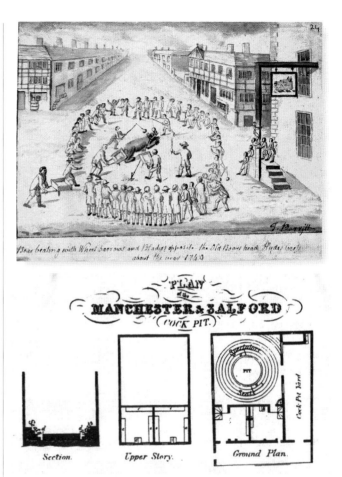

Bear beating with Wheel barrows and Bladers opposite the Old Boars head Hydes Cross about the year 1749

PLAN of the MANCHESTER & SALFORD COCK PIT.

Section.   Upper Story.   Ground Plan.

▲ **Bull and bear baiting** were popular diversions in 18th century Manchester. Shown here in 1749 (*top*) a bear is being baited, unusually, with wheelbarrows and inflated bladders on sticks, outside the Old Boar's Head, Hyde's Cross (where Urbis now stands).

The usual form of baiting was, however, rather more bloody. A stake would be hammered into the ground and the bull or bear, often decked in coloured ribbons, tied up. Dogs would then be incited to attack; their chief ploy being to bite the creature's nose and hang on.

The owner of the dog that survived for longest would win the prize. The bulldog spirit indeed!

The **Manchester and Salford Cock Pit** at Kersal Moor racecourse, as depicted on Twyford and Wilson's map of 1832 (*above*) had bench seats for up to 150 spectators. Two 'Masters of the Match', or umpires, sat on opposite sides of the pit. An upper storey housed pens for the cocks.

The cockpit was one place where all classes mixed relatively freely. One regular to Manchester's pit in the 1820s was the Earl of Derby.

▶ Branding is hardly a modern phenomenon. With its single red rose this cap (on display at the Old Trafford cricket museum) was enough to identify its wearer as a member of the **Lancashire County Cricket Club**. Dating from c.1870 and once worn by the amateur all-rounder, the Rev. Vernon Royle, it is the oldest county cap in existence.

Formed in 1824, **Denton CC** (*right*) once played at a ground called Angel Field. After they moved on in 1860, Cricket Street was built on the site. When a change of its name to Florence Street was mooted 47 years later there were howls of protests. Who prevailed? See the back cover.

In recent years several clubs have adopted US-style tags. For Sale RFC read the Sale Sharks, for Salford RLFC, the Salford Reds. But there is surely no racier title than that of Manchester's speedway favourites, the **Belle Vue Aces**, christened in 1928.

Like many clubs **Manchester City** have often updated their crest, the latest version being on display at Sportcity (*below right*). City were once rebranded too. Before 1887 they were called Ardwick. Elsewhere, Christchurch FC became Bolton Wanderers, while City's rivals spent 24 years as Newton Heath before their new owner decided in 1902 that 'Manchester United' had a better ring to it.

≫ Horse and Jockey laid on the bulls. Brewing interests have long been patrons of sport.

For the privileged few, hunting in the Manchester region can be traced back to at least the early 14th century. Two hunting parks have been identified; at Bradford on the River Medlock, and Alport, in the Castlefield area. There was an enclosed deer park at Blackley, and one at Dunham Park, Trafford, where examples of deer-leaps survive; that is, platforms built on the outer side of walls, allowing deer to enter, but not exit from the park.

The deer park at Bramall Hall, near Cheadle Hulme, now a golf course, was certainly in use in 1577 and is shown also on Burdett's map of Cheshire of 1777, while the ornamental landscapes of Heaton Hall and Platt Hall (both late 18th century), and Wythenshawe Hall (early 19th century), were almost certainly planned to provide cover and habitat for game.

The Traffords of Trafford Hall were keen hunters (*see p22*) as, surprisingly, was Friedrich Engels, who regularly rode with the Cheshire Hunt whilst working in Manchester during the 1850s and 1860s to help support his friend, Karl Marx.

Returning to the medieval period, as in every other part of the country, from the 14th century onwards Manchester's ruling elite exercised strict controls on popular sports, such as hare coursing and dog fighting, but also on such apparently innocuous games as bowls. This was partly because these activities prevented men from honing their archery skills (*see p76*), but also because they were invariably accompanied by gambling and drinking.

In 1561 a Court Leet entry reiterates a 1390 statute that no person 'unless he may dispend 40s of ffre hold' could keep 'eny Greyhounde Dogge or biche or eny hounde such like'.

In 1595 it is ordered that 'No maner of pson or psons shall use eny bowles or bowling within this town... or throw any bowle or bowles about the street or within the towne or Churchyarde'.

Needless to add, no such restrictions applied to the landed gentry within the confines of their own houses. Indeed by the 17th century bowling greens were practically *de rigueur*.

Football was another proscribed activity. Again, this was a matter of public order, since the game – not the eleven-a-side version that would develop in the mid 19th century – was effectively a mob affair played in the street.

So bad was the disorder that Manchester's Court Leet banned the game altogether in 1608. In 1618 there were even two 'offic'rs for ye ffootball', George Richardson and Robarte Boardman. Two further banning orders followed in 1656 and 1657.

Almost a century later even the so-called 'sport of kings' fell foul of the authorities, when the religious essayist John Byrom managed to gather support for a ban on horse racing at Kersal Moor. This lasted 15 years, much to the displeasure of certain members of the local gentry.

Race meetings were undoubtedly the most popular spectator draw of the pre-modern era (unless one counts public hangings as a sport); not because of the racing so much as the carnival atmosphere that an Easter or Whitsuntide race meeting would engender.

One popular event at Kersal Moor, especially for men, was the 'smock' race referred to earlier, in which scantily clad women competed for smocks, tea and other prized comestibles.

Cock fighting was, meanwhile, a relatively orderly form of activity. In fact alongside cricket – first recorded at the Adelphi ground in Salford c.1823 (see p35) – it was the earliest 'sport' to be formally organised between representatives of different counties. Thus in 1786 we read of a 'main' (or match) of cocks at Manchester's Royal Exchange betwixt the gentlemen of Lancashire and Cheshire for £5 a battle and £200 the main. These were high stakes indeed.

Several cockpits are recorded in Manchester; in 1650 near Market Street, in 1730 on Cross Street, and in 1760 at the upper end of Deansgate. Chorlton Green was another regular venue.

19th century sport

In common with all aspects of social and cultural life, the 19th century witnessed key changes in the nation's sporting life.

Baiting was finally banned in 1835, followed by cock fighting in 1849, although the latter carried on in secret locations for many years thereafter.

As the world's first truly industrialised city – the mighty Cottonopolis – Manchester would in time develop all the attributes necessary to develop a deeply rooted sporting culture, starting with the monied classes and gradually filtering down through the social order, at least amongst the male population.

A key factor was urban growth. Manchester's population more than tripled to around 563,000 between 1838 and 1891.

▶ Set up by a former compositor on the *Manchester Guardian*, the publishing firm of E Hulton & Co, the forerunner of the great Hulton newspaper empire, produced two sports titles from its offices on Mark Lane (now absorbed into the Printworks), off Withy Grove.

These were *The Sporting Chronicle*, launched in 1871, and **The Athletic News** in 1875. The latter's first editor was Tom Sutton, founder of the Manchester Athletic Club (see p26). Athletics then was a far more popular spectator sport than football. But not for long.

In April 1888, after an initial gathering of interested parties in London, the world's first Football League was formed at the **Royal Hotel**, on the corner of Market Street and Mosley Street (*right*).

A leading figure during the League's early years was JJ Bentley. At one point Bentley was not only President of the League and chairman of Bolton Wanderers, but also a First Division referee and a contributor to *Athletic News* (often writing up the matches he had just refereed). It was Bentley who persuaded the FA to stage the 1893 Cup Final at the Fallowfield Stadium, which just happened to belong to Tom Sutton's club. (To learn what ensued, see p62).

Without relinquishing any of his roles, Bentley then succeeded Sutton as *Athletic News* editor.

One of his first acts was to bring forward its publication to Monday, thus sparking a huge rise in circulation. By 1897 it was Britain's leading sports paper, selling 230,000 copies a week.

Bentley later became chairman of Manchester United.

Athletic News finally folded in 1930, unable to compete with the dailies, many of whom had also set up offices in the Withy Grove area.

THE FOOTBALL LEAGUE
Was founded on 17th April 1888 at the Royal Hotel which stood on this site.

▲ Until the late 19th century sport was essentially a male preserve, although croquet, then lawn tennis became popular amongst upper and middle class women from the 1850s onwards. An earlier exception, in high society at least, was **archery** (see Chapter 9).

This 1790s worsted and silk jacket, from the **Platt Hall Gallery of English Costume**, has one remaining button bearing the Prince of Wales's motto, *Ich Dien* (I Serve). This confirms it belonged to a member of the Royal British Bowmen, who, despite their name, granted women full membership when they formed in 1787.

Note that the jacket's attached pink sleeves would have allowed greater freedom of movement than conventional clothing, while giving the impression of exposed arms.

» For the newly industrialised workforce, many of them recently arrived immigrants from Scotland, Ireland and Wales, drink offered the main form of escape.

'The entire labouring population of Manchester is without any season of recreation and is ignorant of all amusements, excepting that very small portion which frequents the theatre,' wrote the doctor James Kay in his seminal 1832 report, *The Moral and Physical Condition of the Working Classes Employed in the Cotton Manufacture in Manchester*.

'Healthful recreation is seldom or never taken by the artisans of this town… were parks provided, recreation would be taken with avidity, and one of the results would be better use of the Sunday and a substitution at all other times for the debasing pleasures now in vogue.'

Three developments during the 1840s helped address some of those concerns. After a seven year campaign by the MP Mark Philips, in 1846 Manchester became one of the first municipalities in Britain to provide public parks.

Three sites were purchased and laid out; Queen's Park, Harpurhey; Peel Park, Salford, and Philips Park, Bradford (see right).

In the same year Manchester took its first tentative steps towards the provision of public baths and laundries. This led in 1855 to the construction of the Greengate Baths, Salford, designed by the up and coming Thomas Worthington and seen as the prototype for all baths and pools that followed (see Chapter 17)

A third reform, again enacted after pressure from Manchester politicians, resulted in the lowering of working hours for industrial workers.

The 1847 Factory Act, in particular, gave workers Saturday afternoons off, thus freeing thousands of men to participate in leisure activities, of which sport would grow in importance.

At that time Manchester's only regularly organised spectator sport was cricket, at Broughton and Denton for example, or at the new county ground at Old Trafford, which was conveniently located by one of six commuter railway lines completed during the 1840s, well in advance of any other city. Manchester's omnibus network, started in 1824, was also developed by then.

This network formed a vital component in the development of sport, enabling players and spectators to move around the city, and beyond.

Three main centres of activity emerged at this period. In the north there formed a cluster of attractions around Broughton; for example a zoo, and in 1857, Britain's first Turkish Baths.

In Trafford Park there were two major leisure areas, the Botanical Gardens and exhibition grounds, and Pomona Gardens, which had the largest assembly hall in Britain (see Chapter 2). However the most commercially driven was Belle Vue, where apart from a zoo and amusement park, the Jennison family soon realised the commercial potential of sport, starting with bowls and rabbit coursing, then athletics during the 1880s (see Chapter 4).

As the city's growing middle classes found more disposable income at their fingertips, private sports clubs started to develop around the city, initially for golf, cricket and bowls. The Manchester Football Club (which actually played rugby, although the distinctions then were blurred) formed in Whalley Range in 1860, thus becoming the first club in the north, followed by Sale a year later.

Not only did sport offer healthy activity, but also social bonding. With so many newly arrived

workers in the city, a sports club provided an ideal framework in which to meet friends and, just as importantly, to forge new identities.

Slowly but surely women started to join in, playing croquet from the 1850s, and later, lawn tennis. The Northern Tennis Club formed at Old Trafford in 1881.

Lawn tennis was tailor made for the suburbs. Adapted from the much older game – now known as real tennis (which itself was first played at a new Manchester club in 1876, *see Chapter 11*) – it was one of several sporting activities made possible by technological advancement; namely the invention of the lawnmower in the 1830s, followed by India Rubber in the 1850s. (Only air-filled rubber balls will actually bounce on turf.)

Like archery and croquet before, one of lawn tennis's great advantages was that girls and ladies could play without losing their modesty or perspiring too greatly. Tennis clubs accordingly sprang up in almost every suburb, often in association with existing cricket and bowls clubs.

Best of all the new suburban clubs fitted neatly into the plots of land left vacant in the middle of a grid of four residential streets (*see p71*). They also offered safe environments in which members of the opposite sex could mingle.

Other scientific breakthroughs led to the development of roller skating rinks and, in 1876, in Rusholme, of the first man-made indoor rink outside of London (and indeed only the fourth ever built). Again, rinks were ideal for courtship (*see Chapter 13*).

The availibility of pedal cycles with pneumatic tyres – another benefit of India Rubber – brought even greater freedom. In 1883 an estimated 30,000 spectators were said to have packed Alexandra Park for a cycling rally.

Among several clubs formed during this fecund period of innovation and enterprise were the Manchester Wheelers, the Salford Harriers, the all-conquering Osborne Street Baths Water Polo team, and numerous lacrosse teams, many of them inspired by the visit of two Canadian teams to Longsight in 1876. It is one of least explicable quirks of the local sporting scene that lacrosse should have become more popular in and around Manchester than in any other part of Britain.

By the 1880s sport was a part of the city's social and commercial fabric. Its moral fabric too.

Mens sana in corpore sano was a creed that served a number of diverse interests; employers, politicians, churchmen, teachers, philanthropists, doctors and businessmen alike. »

▲ Parks form a vital element in the public provision of sport. But Manchester is particularly well blessed with parks of historic interest. One of three to open in 1846 was **Philips Park** (opposite Sportcity). Named after the MP Mark Philips, who led the Parks for the Citizens of Manchester Campaign, the park was laid out by Joshua Major of Knowsthorpe and is listed Grade II on the Register of Historic Parks and Gardens.

Under the terms of the original design competition, the park was required to have 'playgrounds' for archery, quoits and skittles. This was at least 30 years before parks football started. A bowling green was laid out in 1872 and is still in use, lovingly tended by two older members of the park's bowls club, while tennis courts appeared in the 1890s. Philips Park also had the city's first open air swimming pool, opened in 1891. Reflecting the changes in sporting trends, there is nowadays a basketball area.

Manchester parks have shed a large number of facilities since 1945. Currently there are 70 tennis courts (compared with 418 in 1927), 35 bowling greens (71), and six cricket pitches (86). The number of football pitches has however risen from 182 to 199.

Lottery funding and a new sense of resolve has, meanwhile, helped rescue Britain's parks from years of decline. Philips Park's once derelict lodge has been restored and a Friends Group set up by local residents. The next target is to win one of the Civic Trust's coveted Green Flag awards, already held by several other parks in the city.

Players Please! The rise of the white collar worker created a new demand for sports facilities in town centres. Based on earlier models in Manhattan, Manchester's YMCA, on Peter Street (left) – designed by Woodhouse, Corbett & Dean and opened in 1911 – offered a top floor swimming pool, gymnasium and running track. None of these **survived the building's conversion to offices in the 1990s. Though rather less handsome, the YMCA's new centre, the Y Club on Liverpool Road, Castlefield, has superb sports facilities, including an 18m pool and, interestingly, two courts for Rugby Fives, a form of handball which used to be played against church walls.**

▲ **Mather and Platt** (now part of the Weir Group), whose Park Works, Newton Heath, are shown (*top*) in 1969, were one of several companies to lay on extensive sports facilities. Tootal Broadhurst Lee's grounds on Ten Acres Lane can be seen at the top of the aerial view. Other companies with sports facilities were Avro, Exide, Ferranti, Renold's and McVitie & Price. The Co-operative Wholesale Society purchased its own sports ground in 1928 at Moston (*see p73*), followed by Metropolitan Vickers, at Finny Bank Lane in 1936. Metro-Vick's sports days at Belle Vue or Fallowfield would draw up to 15,000 spectators in the 1930s.

Some companies even hired former professional sportsmen to coach their teams. During the 1950s Manchester also had a thriving industrial netball league.

Since the 1990s many of the Park Works' buildings, the prominent tower included, have been cleared, and although the bowling green and football pitch survive, the cricket pitch is now sadly overgrown.

Another of Manchester's sporting arenas to have succumbed is the **Hyde Road Stadium**, home of the Belle Vue Aces, demolished in 1988 (*above*). Although starkly utilitarian (*see p46*) its loss is still felt keenly by speedway fans.

>> Involving youths in sport also helped lessen street crime and gang warfare. In 1887, a year after the first Lads' Club was formed, in Hulme (*see Chapter 14*), concerned church leaders in Ardwick formed the club that would later become Manchester City.

Breweries were also quick to latch onto the potential of sport, just as they once been keen to sponsor bull baiting. Castle Irwell racecourse, the successor to Kersal Moor, was described in 1867 as 'a complete canvas city of public houses'. Football offered an even greater opportunity.

Indeed both Manchester City and United were rescued from bankruptcy by brewing interests during their early years. Brewers also saw the potential for incorporating bowling greens (*see Chapter 10*) and billiard tables (*see Chapter 15*) into their pub designs, a trend which the Temperance movement later countered with their own billiard halls (*see p112*) in the Edwardian period.

A split in the rugby world over the payment of players gave rise to another new sport in 1895, that of Northern Union (later renamed rugby league). Manchester had three professional clubs by the early 20th century, with others based in the surrounding towns of Rochdale, Oldham and Wigan. In fact Manchester and Leeds were the only northern cities in which all three football codes – association football, rugby union and rugby league – could be said to have co-existed successfully. In all other cities, most notably Hull and Liverpool, the dominance of one code tended to preclude success for the others.

Such regional variations can often be subtle in form, and intriguing too for historians.

20th century sport

While private clubs thrived in the wealthier districts, such as Broughton and Didsbury, the early 20th century was marked by a substantial increase in the number and type of sports facilities provided by local authorities, educational establishments and large companies (*see left*).

Enriched by the newly opened Ship Canal, in the late 1890s Manchester Corporation set about the construction of five public baths and laundries, the most opulent being the Victoria Baths in Chorlton-cum-Medlock, opened in 1906, the Taj Mahal of British swimming pools (*see pp123-125*).

Of equal national stature, in architectural terms, was the Salford Lads' Club, inaugurated in 1904 (*see pp106-107*), and the magnificent Manchester Ice Palace (*pp97-99*), which from its gala opening in 1910 until the late 1920s was the finest ice rink in Britain and the second largest in Europe, after Berlin. For a decade or more Manchester was the epicentre of British skating.

Equally impressive was the revamped Castle Irwell racecourse, re-opened in 1902 and in every sense the city's first 20th century sports venue, bristling with modern accoutrements.

In a similar vein, Manchester United's new 60,000 capacity stadium at Old Trafford, opened in 1910, was the first truly purpose-built football venue in Britain, as opposed to an adaptation of an existing site. Even then the club was dubbed 'Moneybags United'.

Despite the fact that still no-one was profiting hugely from sport – the breweries excepted – Manchester's ever alert entrepreneurs continually sought new forms of leisure. Billiard halls

were one craze of the early 20th century. Then in 1926 Britain's first stadium for greyhound racing, a sport introduced from America, was built at Belle Vue. This was followed two years later by speedway, invented in Australia.

Three more stadiums were hurriedly erected to capitalise on these new crazes; an added stadium for speedway at Belle Vue, plus greyhound and speedway stadiums at Salford and White City, which itself was a short-lived amusement park on the site of the Botanical Gardens (*see Chapter 2*).

In an urban plan drawn up by Manchester City Council after the Second World War it was reported that the city's 22 parks, 52 recreation areas and 35 small open spaces amounted to only three acres per 1,000 of the city's population, less than half the recognised minimum standard of seven acres per 1,000.

'Unless more playing-fields are made available, local clubs will be forced to travel to sports grounds outside the city boundary; active sports would then be virtually denied to the lowest-paid members of the community, whose need of them is greatest.'

Amongst the proposals were plans for two district sports centres, in Cheetham Hill and at Hough End. Neither was built, and the only major achievement in the immediate post war period was the conversion of Hough End into football and rugby pitches. These are still well used today.

Attendances at sports venues reached unprecedented peaks in the immediate post war period. Gates of 80,000 and more became common at Manchester City's Maine Road. Record attendances were also established at Salford City rugby league club, at Old Trafford cricket ground and at Belle Vue. Manchester United's international fame dates from this period, starting with the rise of the talented 'Busby Babes' in the early 1950s, but tragically fated to immortal status by the Munich disaster of 1958, a key event in the life of the city.

But while in the ensuing decade individuals such as United's George Best came to symbolise the 'Swinging Sixties', the period was also marked by decline. Castle Irwell closed in 1963, leaving Manchester without its own racecourse for the first time since at least 1681, followed by the Ice Palace in 1967. Three of the city's four greyhound and speedway stadiums closed during the 1980s. Cricket at Broughton ceased in 1979, while Swinton rugby league club lost its ground in 1992.

Numerous swimming baths in the city were also closed, the Victoria Baths included, in 1993.

The 20th century ended, as did the 19th century, with a burst of activity in the public sector. The series of Council-led initiatives that led to Manchester hosting the 2002 Commonwealth Games – starting with a bid for the Olympic Games in 1985 and culminating in the creation of an entirely new complex at Sportcity (*see Chapter 5*), plus an indoor arena at Victoria Station and a new water palace for the 21st century on Oxford Road – signalled a new era of public-private partnerships, using sport as a catalyst for urban regeneration.

Every trend and every sport we have mapped briefly here has left its mark in one way or another; either in the form of buildings or sporting landscapes, or in the form of sports clubs and local traditions.

Manchester may have given up baiting bulls and bears. It may also have lost its racecourse, and countless other open spaces to urban sprawl and roads.

But there are still plenty of locals who like a drink and a bet around a bowling green, and still the odd unruly footballer too.

Manchester has a long history of staging international events, one of the earliest being an athletics meeting in 1891 in the grounds of the Botanical Gardens. The buttressed remains of the gardens' original gateway still stand today (*above left*), while in the distance, Old Trafford grows ever larger. United's stadium is quite unrecognisable from the ground that staged matches during the 1966 World Cup. As packed stands at the 2002 Commonwealth Games suggest, Manchester's appetite for top flight sport seems never to diminish.

Chapter Two

Trafford Park

Sir Humphrey de Trafford (1862-1929) was the last family member to occupy Trafford Hall before the sale of the estate in 1896. Like his father, also Sir Humphrey (1808-1886), he was a 'sportsman' in the traditional sense of the word; his passions being fox hunting, big game shooting and horse racing. He wrote books on all three subjects, listing his other interests as polo, lawn tennis, cricket and coursing. His grandfather, Sir Thomas Trafford, had adopted the rather grander surname of 'de Trafford' in 1841 on being made a baronet by Queen Victoria.

Even to people with little knowledge of Manchester, the name Old Trafford is synonymous with sport.

The Old Trafford cricket ground, home of Lancashire County Cricket Club, has staged Test Matches since 1884, whilst a short walk northwards looms the massive presence of the Old Trafford football stadium, headquarters of arguably the most famous sports club on the planet, Manchester United.

What is much less known is that the Trafford Park area was a focus for sport long before United moved there in 1910. At least *eighteen* different sports are recorded as having been staged in the area since the 18th century, including athletics, golf, polo, horse racing, curling and rowing.

This concentration is simply explained. Moreover, it provides a perfect illustration of how clusters of sports venues – as found in several British cities – often occur as the result of a shared former land use and/or ownership.

In the case of Trafford Park, before the wholesale transformation of the landscape by the creation of the Manchester Ship Canal and the Trafford Park Industrial Estate at the end of the 19th century, the area fell largely within the boundaries of one private estate, owned since the 11th century by the Trafford family.

Trafford Park's unified ownership, its level topography, its proximity to the centres of Manchester and Salford, and the presence of the River Irwell, provided ideal conditions for the evolution of what we would now call a sports and leisure zone.

Certainly when Sir Humphrey de Trafford finally put the estate on the market in the 1890s – the Ship Canal having rather lessened its charms – Manchester Corporation's Open Spaces Committee did consider buying it for parkland and development.

Given his family's strong leanings towards sport over the years this is apparently what Sir Humphrey would have preferred.

But in the end the Corporation demurred and the park's 1183 acres, including Trafford Hall (the family seat since the 17th century),

a deer park, stables, a glass house, four farms and three lodges, were sold in 1896 to a bidder with only profit in mind.

Ernest Hooley, a flamboyant speculator, paid £360,000 sight unseen for the bulk of Trafford Park. Within fifteen years over 40 large companies had moved in – Westinghouse, the CWS and Ford Motors included – requiring a vast supporting infrastructure of roads, railways and housing, all of which completely and utterly obliterated the area's pastoral character.

A century later, only three of the area's pre-1914 sports venues remain; the cricket ground, the football stadium and a bowls club.

But as the map opposite shows, they are the mere remnants of what was once considered a sporting paradise.

For example, in 1898, as work began on the creation of the industrial estate – the first of its type in the world – the 80 acre **Trafford Park Golf Course** (*map ref* 2) was laid out immediately to the south of **Trafford Hall** (1), which itself became the headquarters of the **Manchester Golf Club.** »

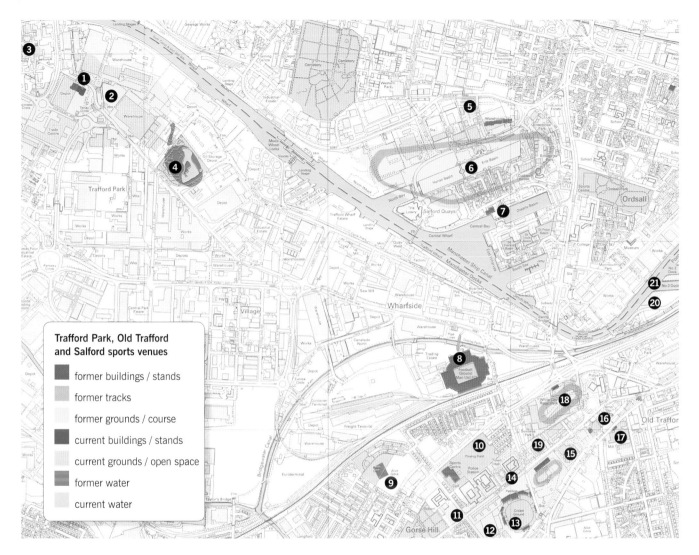

1. **Trafford Hall** (c.1760-1945)
2. **Trafford Park golf course** (1898-1914)
3. **Trafford Park polo grounds** (c.1880s)
4. **Boating lake**, now Trafford Ecology Park (mid C19-)
5. **New Barns rugby ground** (1878-1901)
6. **New Barns racecourse** (1867-1901)
7. **Salford Quays Watersport Centre** (1999-)
8. **Old Trafford football stadium** (1910-)
9. **Curling pond** (up to c.1914)
10. **Stretford Leisure Centre** (1977-)
11. **Old Trafford polo ground / M/cr Police sports ground** (c.1880s - c.1930)
12. **Gun Club** (c.1880s-1898)
13. **Old Trafford cricket ground** (1856-)
14. **Southern Cricket Ground** and **Clifford Cricket Ground** (c.1880s-1930)
15. **Manchester Cricket Club ground** (1847-56) and **Manchester Athletic Club** (1887-91)
16. **Old Trafford Bowling Club** (1877-) *see p83*
17. **Northern Lawn Tennis Club** (1881-1908)
18. **Botanical Society Gardens** (1827-1907) and **White City Amusement Park** (1907-28) and **White City Stadium** (1928-87)
19. **1887 Jubilee Exhibition site**
20. **Pomona Gardens** (c.1840-88)
21. **Regatta course** (1842-51)

MANCHESTER REGATTA—FROM A SKETCH BY MR. HAYES.

▲ To sketch the 1844 **Manchester Regatta** (*map ref 21*) for the *Illustrated London News,* the artist positioned himself where the Irwell takes a sharp turn at Throstle Nest Bridge, and looked north eastwards towards the distant cathedral.

Manchester's earliest rowing club was the Clarence, formed in 1828, followed by Nemesis, who in 1850 built a boathouse at Cornbrook, located just past the grandstand (*shown above right*).

Inspired by their lead and by the crews from across Britain who competed in the regattas, another 15 rowing clubs formed in the city over the following decade.

Gambling and race-fixing eventually led to rowing's demise, while pollution forced Manchester's rowers upstream to Agecroft, where regattas continued under the auspices of **Agecroft Rowing Club** until 1997. A build up of plantlife in that area – due, ironically, to the lack of pollution – then forced Agecroft to return downriver in 1999 (*see p34*).

》 West of the golf course, between the Bridgewater Canal and Ashburton Road, an **airfield** operated from 1910-18. In 1911 it was a staging post for the *Daily Mail* Round Britain air race.

As respectable members of the landed gentry, the de Traffords were naturally keen equestrians. The second baronet was Master of the Trafford Harriers and hunted in the estate grounds until at least the 1860s. The records of the **Manchester Polo Club** – England's first provincial club (now merged with other clubs and based in Cheshire) – also confirm that the third baronet played polo in the 1880s, when the Queen's Bays cavalry regiment was quartered at Hulme Barracks.

Two area of Trafford Park (*3 and 11*) were set aside at different periods for polo, a sport imported from the Indian sub-continent by army officers in the 1870s.

But what the de Traffords thought of the arrival of a race-course on the northern border

of their estate in 1867 we do not know. The family had already sponsored the Stretford Handicap, held in 1841 and from 1852-54 on the site of what would become the Old Trafford Cricket Ground.

But regular race meetings with regular crowds was quite another matter. Indeed the only reason Manchester's Race Committee bought the 100 acre site at New Barns (*6*) was because the owner of the previous course at Castle Irwell (*see p33*) had refused to countenance any more gambling and drinking on his property.

The **New Barns Racecourse** (*6*) – now the Lowry Centre site – was not ideal. Laid out on marshy ground, one observer, Charles Richardson, wrote that at times the going was 'so rotten as to be absolutely dangerous.' He added, 'The drive through squalid and dirty streets is not invigorating... (but) the unsavoury slums of Salford are quickly forgotten when one passes through the gate into the flower-bedizened paddock,

with its trim footpaths and sparkling fountains.'

For a few years New Barns caught racegoers' imagination by offering an £11,000 pot for the Lancashire Plate, making it Britain's most lucrative race.

Another high point was the visit in 1888 of Colonel Cody's 'Buffalo Bill' Wild West Show – a show which toured Britain's sports grounds and parks with huge success, spreading cowboy mania amongst the youth of the day.

In 1898 the Ship Canal company decided it needed New Barns as the site of its proposed Number Nine dock, and by 1902, Castle Irwell had once again became the focus of Manchester racing.

Back at Trafford Park, the next sport on offer was **curling** and **skating,** on a pond (*9*), where the Burleigh Road allotments now lie. A report in *The Sphinx* in 1871 describes a gathering attended by some 150 people and mentions the second baronet, Sir Humphrey, as both a patron and a keen player.

There were two substantial pleasure gardens in Old Trafford during the Victorian period.

On the Irwell's banks, opposite Ordsall Hall, stood **Pomona Gardens** (20, *see right*), from c.1840-88, while across Chester Road was the **Botanical Gardens** (18), opened in the 1820s.

Compared with Manchester's other fleeting attractions – the Vauxhall Gardens in Collyhurst, or the Manchester Zoological Gardens, Higher Broughton – and also compared with Belle Vue (*see Chapter 4*), the headquarters of the Botanical Society were by far the most exclusive, and expensive of all Manchester's gardens. It only opened occasionally for non-members, and had numerous influential patrons (the de Traffords included). Entrance was via a suitably imposing neo-classical lodge on Chester Road, opposite the southern gates of the Trafford park estate.

There would be five important sports venues and two major exhibitions built within or close to the Botanical Gardens' boundaries during the period 1847-1928.

The first of these was the ground of the **Manchester Cricket Club**, the forerunner of Lancashire CCC. This club, the first cricket club recorded in the city, had formed as Aurora CC some time between 1818-23, on the Adelphi Ground, Salford (*see p35*), and had latterly been based on Moss Lane, Moss Side. When that ground was required for the construction of St Mary's church, in 1847 the club rented land (15) at the rear of the Botanical Gardens at the invitation of Sir Thomas de Trafford.

The timing of their arrival was fortuitous for two reasons.

Firstly, in 1847, thanks largely to the agitation of Manchester men,

the new Factory Act gave greater numbers of industrial workers time off on Saturday afternoons. Cricket was thus opened up to a wider audience. Then in 1849 the completion of the Manchester-Altrincham railway (the city's first commuter line), with Old Trafford station close by, made the Manchester Cricket Club ground at least as accessible as Belle Vue.

But the club was not allowed to settle. When it was decided that Manchester should emulate London's Crystal Palace with a great exhibition of its own – the 1857 exhibition of Art Treasures – the de Traffords offered the cricket ground as the site.

But the cricketers were well compensated for their inconvenience. In addition to receiving £1,300, the de Traffords leased them a larger plot only a few hundred yards westwards along the railway line. As mentioned earlier, the site had previously been used to stage the Stretford Steeplechase, during the 1840s and 1850s. Now it would become the **Old Trafford Cricket Ground** we know today (13).

But the Art Treasures Exhibition was not the end of sport on the Botanical Gardens site.

Thirty years after the cricket club departed, it was selected once again for a major event, the 1887 Royal Jubilee Exhibition. This time two large iron and glass exhibition halls were built on either side of Talbot Road (which itself had only recently been laid and ran only as far as Warwick Road).

And for all its fine halls and worthy content, as many exhibition and pleasure garden operators of the period were discovering, one of the most potent magnets to draw in audiences was sport. »

THE ROYAL POMONA PALACE, MANCHESTER.
SOUTH WEST VIEW FROM THE RIVER.

▲ Named after the Roman goddess of fruit trees – no doubt because it staged produce and agricultural shows – surprisingly little is known about the **Pomona Gardens** (*20*), which was created on the site of the Cornbrook Strawberry Gardens some time in the 1840s. Indeed this undated sketch printed by the firm of John Heywood's of Deansgate and Ridgefield, is the best representation we have.

Yet it was clearly a major enterprise.

Three sizeable exhibition halls dominated the site, one of which, the Great Hall, was reckoned to be the largest indoor space in Britain, measuring 45,800 sq.ft and reputedly able to hold 28,000 people. Disraeli twice addressed gatherings there.

In November 1878, Pomona's sports ground staged Manchester's second ever floodlit football match, under Siemens lights (the first having taken place at Broughton a month earlier, *see p42*). One of the teams involved was the forerunner of Salford City Reds, **Cavendish,** who were then based at a field on the opposite bank of the Irwell, in front of Ordsall Hall. As Salford, the

club would later move to a ground called **New Barns** (5), next to the **racecourse** of the same name (6).

Pomona also staged wrestling, gymnastics and 'other engaging displays of manly strength and athletic skill'.

A devastating explosion at a neighbouring chemical works in 1887 (perhaps the building shown in the top left), and, no doubt, the success of that year's Royal Jubilee Exhibition at the nearby Botanical Gardens, led to the closure of the Pomona Gardens a year later.

But of course the name lives on. The Pomona Docks were built on the site as part of the Ship Canal works in the late 1890s, and there is the Pomona Metrolink stop, which is on the same line as the railway shown above.

▲ These photographs show the south west elevation of **Trafford Hall** (*map ref 1*), built in Adams-style in the 1760s on the side of an earlier 16th century house.

The Hall's construction coincided with the first incursion of industry to this part of Manchester, namely the completion of the Bridgewater Canal, which cut through both the eastern and western corners of the Trafford's family estate.

The top image dates from the period 1898-1914, when part of Trafford Hall – abandoned by Sir Humphrey a few years earlier when the Ship Canal opened – served as a clubhouse for **Manchester Golf Club**. Reduced subscriptions were offered to encourage white collar workers from the neighbouring industrial estate to join up. But as the air grew more polluted, in 1912 the club decamped to Hopwood. The Hall was then purchased by Arthur Guinness & Co. and rented to the newly formed **Trafford Park Golf Club**.

By 1934, as the lower image graphically illustrates, industry dominated. Note the Hall's blackened masonry. On the right is the soap works of Thomas Hedley & Co, opened in 1933.

Trafford Hall was badly damaged during the same night of bombing in December 1940 which also wrecked Old Trafford football ground, and was demolished soon after the war.

It stood 150m north of where Tenax Circle is now located.

» Also in 1887, for example, over at Belle Vue, an athletics ground was prepared for the use by the emerging Salford Harriers. At the same time Ardwick FC (later Manchester City) moved into an enclosed ground off Hyde Road. Pomona Gardens, which had its own sports field, closed meanwhile, after an explosion in the neighbouring chemical works.

And so it was decided that Old Trafford should have an athletics venue of its own.

Laid out on the western side of the former cricket ground, immediately adjoining the Jubilee Exhibition site, with a quarter mile cinder track and a single grandstand backing onto Talbot Road, Old Trafford's newest venue (15) became the home of the newly formed **Manchester Athletic Club**.

This largely elite club had been set up by Tom Sutton, editor of *Athletic News* (*see* p17), at a time when quasi-professional 'pedestrianism' – which attracted large crowds and heavy betting – was seen as a direct threat to the amateur ethos of true 'athletes'.

The club nevertheless offered cash prizes at its opening meeting in June 1887, and was no doubt delighted when crowds of up to 10,000 attended subsequent meetings. A further indication of the Old Trafford track's calibre, or at least Sutton's clout, was its selection to host the prestigious Amateur Athletic Association's championships on June 27 1891, an event which featured top athletes from New York and, according to *Athletic News*, 'caused a wonderful amount of interest.'

Alas, however, 'wretchedly wet weather' from 9 o'clock to 3 o'clock in the afternoon 'upset all calculations' and only 5,000 spectators turned up.

Still, the Americans were well received and at a dinner held at the Botanical Gardens thanked their hosts. 'It was not more than a century ago,' said Eugene Van Schaik from Manhattan, 'that our two nations were at war, trying to cut each other's throats.' But now the war had been changed to the more peaceful one of athletics.

'Hear hear' came the response. But with developers waiting in the wings, the event proved to be the track's last. Sutton argued for the club to stay in the area – this was prior to Trafford Park's industrialisation – but other Manchester AC members settled instead for £150 in compensation and a new site on Whitworth Lane, Fallowfield (*see* p62).

Before leaving this corner of Old Trafford, two other sites must be mentioned.

In 1877 a section of the former cricket ground was purchased by the newly formed **Old Trafford Bowling Club** (16), whose substantial Tudoresque pavilion can still be seen on Talbot Road (*see* p83). It is one of Old Trafford's, and Manchester's least known sporting gems.

Four years later, on the other side of the Manchester-Altrincham railway, and within an easy lob of the bowls club, the **Northern Lawn Tennis Club** (17) was established, with Sir Humphrey as its first president. Twenty-two courts were laid out and a half-timbered pavilion erected for £375.

The club's annual Northern Tournament (alternated with the Aigburth Club in Liverpool until 1928), would become one of the prime events in Manchester's sporting calendar.

However, as the Old Trafford area became increasingly polluted, in 1908 the members decided to

move to the leafier surrounds of Didsbury, where their wooden pavilion was re-erected and where the club remains until this day.

Tennis Street, off Seymour Grove, is the sole surviving token of the club's sojourn here.

A change in the air, or was it simply public taste, also led to the sale of the Botanical Gardens to two businessmen, Messrs Heathcote and Brown, who reopened the site as the **White City Amusement Park**.

(White City was a name first coined for the grounds of the 1893 World Columbian Exposition in Chicago, for which all the pavilions were painted white. London borrowed the title and the colour scheme too, for its Franco-British exhibition and Olympic Stadium of 1908.)

Manchester's own White City looked set for glory. On its first day in May 1907 it drew 32,972 visitors. But it would soon have a counter-attraction.

As *Athletic News* commented in March 1909: 'The west of Manchester is destined to be the Mecca of sportsmen of that great commercial city. "To the West,

to the West!" will be the cry of our football folks when leaves are falling next autumn. Already we have the Lancashire County Cricket ground, the Northern Lawn Tennis Club, the Manchester Gun Club, the Polo ground, the curling pond, the Manchester Golf Club and numerous other organisations of similar character, devoted to pastime and recreation...'

Until then, **Manchester United** had played at Bank Street (*see p52*), not far from their rivals City, or from White City's long established rival, Belle Vue.

But now they were come to Old Trafford, and to a massive ground (8) that not only heralded a new phase in stadium design but one that would in time become synonymous with the area.

There had been earlier sporting fads. But none as all-consuming as professional football.

White City's prospects suddenly looked bleak. Hit first by the outbreak of war in 1914, then by the Depression, the bulk of its rides and attractions were cleared in 1928 to make way for one more stab at commercial success. »

▶ Now curiously detached, in every sense of the word, on the edge of the White City retail park (*right*), the Grade II listed gateway on Chester Road originally formed the entrance of the **Botanical Gardens**. Built in 1827 the gates later served the **White City Amusement Park**, created in 1907 (*top*), and from 1928-81, the **White City Greyhound Stadium** (*18*). Amongst White City's many attractions was a roller skating rink (seen to the right of the stadium in the 1970s aerial view, *above left*). From 1909-11 this was used by the White City Roller Hockey Club.

In the top left of the aerial view is the **Old Trafford Bowling Club** (*16, see p83*), while to the right of the green is an open field where

the **1887 Jubilee Exhibition** was staged. To the right of this are houses built on the area where the **Manchester Athletics Club** was based from 1887-91. These have since made way for the offices and car parks of Kellogg's.

The bowls club is thus the only patch of green left from this corner of the Trafford Park estate which from 1847 provided a base for so many sporting activities.

» And so to Old Trafford's third major venue, the 40,000 capacity **White City Greyhound and Speedway Stadium** (*above, on the right*). But it was already a crowded market. Salford had just opened a similar stadium (*see p42*), while Belle Vue had a stadium each for these two newly invented sports. So although White City's new stadium was spacious, well-equipped, offered plenty of cover and had good transport links, it always struggled to earn its keep. Speedway failed within a year. Stock car racing, occasional rugby and amateur football matches were staged subsequently. A cinder track added in 1953 was briefly graced by elite athletes such as Emil Zatopek and Gordon Pirie. But White City ended its days as an echoing dog track in October 1981, and was finally demolished in the 1990s to make way for the White City Retail Park.

Amid the car parks and fast foot outlets, only the Botanical Gardens gates were left standing.

And yet, how fitting that possibly Old Trafford's oldest structure should be the sole remnant of an area whose purpose has for so long been to provide pleasure for the people of Manchester.

They appear to be a gateway to nowhere, and yet in truth offer a fascinating doorway into history.

▲ Car parks, retail parks, industrial parks and business parks where once there were real parks, gardens, racecourses, polo grounds and open spaces. Spot the difference – Old Trafford and Trafford Park in 1932 (*above left*) and again in 2002 (*above*).

As all cricket buffs know, the two streets immediately north of Trafford Town Hall (seen in mid-construction opposite) are named after Lancashire's illustrious opening batsmen of the late 19th century, AN Hornby and Dick Barlow. Of the pair, the Preston poet Francis Thompson famously wrote, whilst watching a match at Lord's in the early 1900s:

'For the field is full of shades as I near the shadowy coast,
And a ghostly batsman plays to the bowling of a ghost,
And I look through my tears on a soundless clapping host,

As the run-stealers flicker to and fro,
to and fro:
O my Hornby and my Barlow long ago...'

Shadows and ghosts... Amid the cantilevered stands and plastic seats of the new Old Trafford, these never seem far from the surface; especially when you know where to stop, and listen out for the echoes of Trafford Park's own distant, clapping host.

▲ Completed in 1895 at a cost of £12,000, the pavilion at **Old Trafford Cricket Ground** was designed by Thomas Muirhead, architect also of the pavilion at The Oval. Despite many alterations (and bomb damage sustained during the blitz), the building maintains its original layout, with a central viewing area which backs onto the Long Room (behind the arched ground floor windows), flanked by first floor viewing balconies for the players of each team.

When Lancashire County Cricket Club's predecessors, the Manchester Cricket Club,

first rented the ground from Sir Humphrey de Trafford in 1857 there were three separate pavilions, for members and amateur players, for professionals (on the opposite side of the ground), and for Ladies. Women were finally allowed into the main pavilion in 1977 (still some 25 years before Lord's).

Even in this new pavilion the amateurs still received preferential treatment, however, being supplied with three baths compared with only one for the professionals, who were more numerous.

Three years after the pavilion's completion Lancashire purchased

the ground from Sir Humphrey for £24,732. It would prove to be sound business, for the sale of various outlying plots of the site has kept the club afloat throughout many a lean time.

One indication of how modern safety and amenity levels have affected cricket grounds is that whereas Old Trafford once held 46,000 spectators, for the Roses match in 1926, nowadays, within the same space it holds just 19,000. But one aspect of Old Trafford never changes, and that is the ringing of the pavilion bell (*left*) to signal the start of play.

◀ When the Bolton-born Lancashire and England batsman and slow bowler, Dick Barlow (1851-1919), was awarded a benefit match in 1886, he decided to spend some of the proceeds on the creation of a large stained glass window, which he designed himself. (He later designed his own gravestone. 'Bowled at Last' read the inscription.)

The window, completed in 1887, shows Barlow (*right*) with his fellow opening bat at Old Trafford, AN Hornby (1847-1925), an Old Harrovian who won England caps for both cricket and rugby and was a powerful presence in Manchester sporting circles.

Behind the third figure, the Lancashire and England wicket keeper, Richard Pilling, is the original Old Trafford pavilion (*left*) and the Ladies Pavilion (*right*).

For years no-one knew of the window's whereabouts, so in the late 1960s the Lancashire CCC historian and museum curator, Keith Hayhurst, resolved to track it down. One day, making enquiries in Blackpool – where Barlow is buried – Hayhurst spotted a bowls player with a bag bearing the initials LBW.

Leslie Barlow Wilson, as Hayhurst had surmised, was the great man's grandson. Yet neither he nor any of the family seemed keen to discuss the window.

Barlow, it transpired, had fathered an illegitimate son, who had bought the window from Barlow's daughter.

After seven more years on the case, Hayhurst finally found both the owner and the window – as vivid as the day it had been unveiled – in a house in Southport.

It now takes pride of place in the Old Trafford Long Room; a unique memorial to three of Lancashire and England's finest.

▼ Whatever one's view of its architectural merits, Manchester United's **Old Trafford** is probably the most recognised landmark in the city (although it lies within Trafford Metropolitan Borough). With its fine museum the stadium is also one of Manchester's prime tourist destinations.

The experience of visiting Old Trafford demonstrates how complex are the elements which comprise our notion of sporting heritage.

Celebrity is perhaps the most potent of Old Trafford's associations. Then there is the power of place; not only the fact that this is where great events have occurred, but also the sheer physicality of the structures and the financial muscle they express.

Old Trafford is, in this respect, no less a seat of power than Trafford Hall was for many centuries.

Indeed its sway is all the more powerful for being hard earned. Since the stadium opened in 1910, it should be noted, United have not always been high achievers.

Stadiums are often casually likened to cathedrals or shrines, but at Old Trafford three memorials positioned on the stadium's eastern approach evoke genuine reverence.

Phillip Jackson's bronze figure of **Sir Matt Busby** (1909-94), framed by the vast glazed curtain wall of the East Stand (*below left*), honours United's former manager who, after a career as a player with Manchester City, Liverpool and Scotland, oversaw the transformation of United into a European and worldwide legend during the 1950s and 1960s.

The son of Lanarkshire miner, Busby is portrayed at the time of United's European Cup triumph of 1968, a decade after he narrowly survived the Munich air crash.

A memorial to that tragic, seminal moment in the history of United – and of Manchester, and football generally – is displayed on a wall of the East Stand (*below*). Seven of the 'Busby Babes' and 14 other individuals (including club officials and local press men) died on that fateful night in 1958.

A Munich memorial clock can also be seen on the south eastern corner of the stadium.

Legends in sport arise from any number of diverse triumphs or tragedies. But few are as embedded into the fabric of a club or a city as Munich is in Manchester.

And all this before one even enters the cauldron...

▲ With a capacity of over 68,000, **Old Trafford** is Britain's largest club stadium. However the addition of two upper tier quadrants flanking the North Stand (seen on the far side of the pitch) will raise that total to nearer 75,000, and also, fortunately, alleviate the hitherto uneven appearance of the bowl.

Old Trafford is unusual in that whereas the norm at British football venues has been for piecemeal design, using different architects on a stand-per-stand basis, its own development has always followed a masterplan. There have been three of these masterplans since the stadium opened in February 1910.

The first, by the country's leading stadium designer Archibald Leitch (*see p130*), was for an 80,000 capacity stadium costing £60,000 and bankrolled by United's chairman, the brewer JH Davies. It was at the time the most advanced stadium ever conceived in Britain. Indeed it proved to be too ambitious for United's purse and was never completed (although nearly 77,000 once squeezed in for an FA Cup semi-final in 1939).

Leitch's multi-span South Stand (*seen in the 1930s aerial view on p28*) was bombed in 1941.

United's second masterplan was by architects Atherden Nutter in the 1960s. Ernest Atherden had designed one of the country's first cantilevered roof stands at Castle Irwell racecourse (*see p.40*).

Based on similar principles, from 1965-94 all four sides of Old Trafford were redeveloped into a seamless bowl holding 44,600. It would have been more but for the all-seater rule introduced following the 1989 Hillsborough disaster.

Within a year of its completion the same architects, now called Atherden Fuller Leng, started on the third and current masterplan. This began in 1995 with the erection of the £19 million North Stand, whose 58.5m span cantilevered roof, visible right across Trafford Park, is the largest in the world.

Only one element of the original stadium survives, and that is the now disused players' tunnel in the centre of the South Stand.

Chapter Three

Irwell Valley

Pubs often provide clues in the hunt for sporting heritage. Before the building was demolished in 2004, this sign for the Kersal, on Moor Lane (*map ref. 4*) was a reminder that for over 150 years Manchester's main racecourse lay opposite. Known formerly as the Turf Tavern, the pub was a meeting point for the sports fraternity long after the course closed. Agecroft Rowing Club often met there and, in 1884, it was the starting point for the first race of the Salford Harriers.

If the cluster of sports venues located in the Trafford Park area may be attributed largely to the patronage of the de Trafford family, the cluster we now turn to in the Irwell Valley evolved largely for topographical reasons.

Forming the core of this cluster are large expanses of land straddling the meandering course of the Irwell; land that has remained as undeveloped open space simply because the risk of flooding is too great to warrant concentrated development.

But that in itself is not the reason why, unlike Trafford Park, no senior sports venues remain in use within the valley today. Instead, the downturn of industry, combined with sweeping changes to the area's demographics – not least the decline of the once middle-class enclave around Broughton – have, to an extent, led to the area's marginalisation.

In a sporting context therefore, this is an area blighted by loss.

Yet in heritage terms, the Irwell Valley remains one of the city's most rewarding areas for study and for visiting, particularly in conjunction with the recently launched Irwell Sculpture Trail, which takes in several of the sites mentioned here, as well as the stadium-inspired Arena sculpture (*map ref. 21*), by the American artist, Rita McBride (*see also p11*).

An obvious starting point is the river itself.

As explained earlier, as a result of the Manchester Regatta no fewer than 17 rowing clubs formed in the mid 19th century, of which twelve operated on the Irwell, and of which only one survives; the **Agecroft Rowing Club,** formed by Ishmael Lythgoe in the riverside boiler house of a dye works in 1861. This makes Agecroft one of the oldest open membership rowing clubs in the world.

Open membership had its drawbacks, however, as Agecroft's members struggled to strike a balance between the elitist edicts of the sport's governing body – dominated by amateur gentlemen and university graduates who refused to race against any working men – and their own inclination to compete locally against such clubs as Bolton and Ringley, whose crews included, horror of horrors, coal miners.

This snobbery, plus the growth of commercial traffic on the Irwell, and its attendant pollution, caused a decline in the sport by the end of the 19th century.

Agecroft rowed on, all the same, organising annual regattas from the 1860s until 1997 on a course measured from just above the weir by Littleton Bridge to the riverside gardens of Kersal Cell, a former monastery (now demolished) on the eastern bank of the Irwell.

Like most rowing clubs, Agecroft's boathouses were fairly utilitarian. The first, by the start of the regatta course, was on Irwell Street, by the present day Jubilee Bridge. In 1935 they then built a new boathouse (*map ref. 1*) by the end point of the regatta course, on what is now called – somewhat dramatically, given the calm of the river – Whitewater Drive.

Alas in recent years Agecroft has had to abandon racing on this stretch of the river as, ironically, reduced pollution has led to a build up of weeds. The club is now based at Salford Quays (*see p21*). »

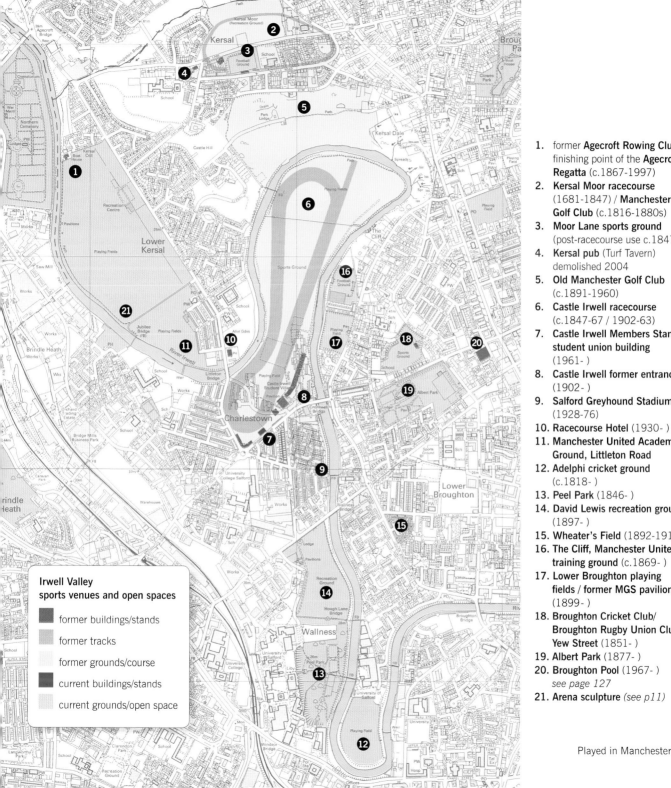

1. former **Agecroft Rowing Club**/ finishing point of the **Agecroft Regatta** (c.1867-1997)
2. **Kersal Moor racecourse** (1681-1847) / **Manchester Golf Club** (c.1816-1880s)
3. **Moor Lane sports ground** (post-racecourse use c.1847-)
4. **Kersal pub** (Turf Tavern) demolished 2004
5. **Old Manchester Golf Club** (c.1891-1960)
6. **Castle Irwell racecourse** (c.1847-67 / 1902-63)
7. **Castle Irwell Members Stand**/ student union building (1961-)
8. **Castle Irwell former entrance** (1902-)
9. **Salford Greyhound Stadium** (1928-76)
10. **Racecourse Hotel** (1930-)
11. **Manchester United Academy Ground, Littleton Road**
12. **Adelphi cricket ground** (c.1818-)
13. **Peel Park** (1846-)
14. **David Lewis recreation ground** (1897-)
15. **Wheater's Field** (1892-1913)
16. **The Cliff, Manchester United training ground** (c.1869-)
17. **Lower Broughton playing fields** / former MGS pavilion (1899-)
18. **Broughton Cricket Club**/ **Broughton Rugby Union Club, Yew Street** (1851-)
19. **Albert Park** (1877-)
20. **Broughton Pool** (1967-) *see page 127*
21. **Arena sculpture** *(see p11)*

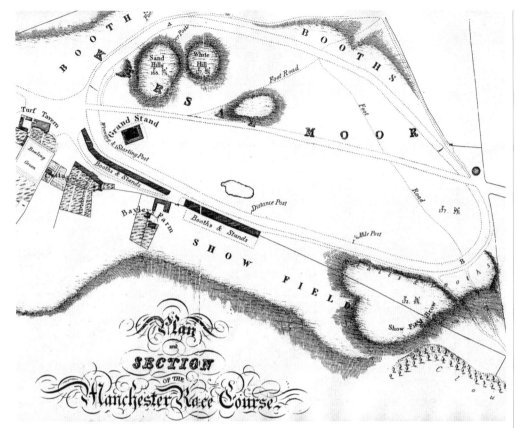

Twyford & Wilson's map of Kersal Moor racecourse (*map ref. 2*), hillocks and all, shows that the southern section of the track corresponds to the route of present day Nevile Road, while the infield to the south is the location of the Moor Lane sports ground. Indeed the etching from 1830 (*right*) would have been drawn from almost exactly the spot occupied by the current stand at Moor Lane, shown opposite. The stand illustrated here was built in 1819, and in 1825 was the scene of an accident when a railing collapsed, injuring numerous spectators. One onlooker also died in 1805 when horses ran out of control.

>> From Agecroft's former base it is a short distance to **Kersal Moor** (*map ref. 2*). Only the rough and hilly section of Kersal Moor, north of Moor Lane, remains as public open space, having been purchased by Salford Corporation in 1937 and more recently designated as a site of biological interest. But the moor is a site of sporting interest too. For over 160 years it was the main racecourse for Manchester.

To digress for a moment, the earliest known race meetings in Manchester were on Barlow Moor, first recorded in 1647, and again from 1697-1701. Racecourses then were often impromptu affairs, requiring only a few ropes and rails, canvas booths and the odd wooden grandstand to be set up on a temporary basis.

According to the *Racing Calendar* there would be short-lived courses or one-off steeplechases at Heaton Park (1827-38), Eccles (1839), Stretford (on the site of the current county cricket ground, 1841 and 1852-54), Gorton Hall (1844-46), Harpurhey (1845), Blackley (1847), Swinton (1876), and the Old Trafford Polo Club (1876).

But from 1681-1847 'Carsall-Moore near Manchester,' as the *London Gazette* of May 1687 described it, was the city's prime venue. And not only for racing.

At the 1681 meeting, for example, according to a local minister a race took place between 'slightly clad women'. This would have been a 'smock race,' commonly staged at racecourses, wakes and fairs, offering prizes such as smocks, tea and sugar for the winner, and undoubted titilation for the spectators.

There was also a cockpit (*see* p15), and a whole series of licensed drinking booths.

Unlicensed 'sutlers and hucksters' were specifically excluded, but no-one could prevent packs of pedlars, prostitutes and thieves from converging on the Moor when the races began, every Whitsuntide.

Kersal Moor was an odd course all the same, particularly as it had three hillocks in the centre. These presumably offered excellent vantage points, but prevented spectators elsewhere following each race in its entirety. But then not everyone was there to follow the races, and somehow the site managed to accommodate crowds estimated at around 100,000. (For a Chartist rally on Kersal Moor in 1838 it was claimed over 300,000 were in attendance.)

Unsurprisingly local church leaders vehemently opposed race meetings, one of them being Dr John Byrom, who penned the hymn *Christians Awake* in nearby Kersal Cell. After considerable lobbying Byrom and his allies finally succeeded in banning meetings at Kersal Moor in 1745.

But not for long.

Not least because the races retained the support of large numbers of the landed gentry, who sponsored most of Britain's horses and jockeys, Kersal Moor was back in action by 1760.

Amongst its influential supporters was Ashton Lever of Alkrington Hall, whom we shall meet later in the chapter on archery, while a race card from 1798 names the race stewards as Humphrey Trafford (of Trafford Hall) and Samuel Clowes.

The Clowes part-owned the land on which the course was laid out and much of the land around the Irwell Valley besides. But eventually even this family's tolerance faded and when »

▲ Easily missed, barely developed, and yet the **Moor Lane** sports ground (*map ref 3*) has remained in use for organised sport for over 320 years; longer, it is thought, than any open space in Manchester. As the map opposite shows, the ground once formed part of Kersal Moor racecourse, which dates back to 1681. From 1847-1919 it was called **Kersal Cricket Ground**. But in 1881 it also staged the **Northern Tennis Tournament** (now played at Didsbury). This was the Northern's second year, the first having been held at Broughton CC (*18*).

Moor Lane was used also from around 1780-1870 by the **Broughton Archers**, and in 1887 for a meeting of the newly-formed **Manchester Athletics Club**, which would later move to Fallowfield.

In 1919 Moor Lane became the home of the **Manchester Football Club**, the city's oldest rugby club (despite the tag FC), formed in 1860. It was during its tenure, in the 1930s, that the concrete post and beam stand seen above, was built. Although of no particular merit architecturally, the use of concrete in the context of a small ground is unusual, and therefore just a little intriguing.

Manchester FC moved on in 1968 (they are now based in Cheadle), and were briefly replaced by **Langworthy Juniors**, an amateur rugby league club. They in turn were followed by the present custodians, **Salford City FC**, who have maintained Moor Lane since 1976 on a lease from Salford City Council. City attract gates of 200-400, although their largest gate was 3,000 for a cup tie in 1981.

More recently, from 2002-04 the ground was also rented by **Swinton Rugby League Club**.

Moor Lane might therefore appear a typical amateur sports ground, but it is in truth an historic sporting landscape which merits both acknowledgement, and, lest we forget, thanks to those volunteers who work so hard to keep it in trim.

>> the Manchester Racecourse Committee's lease finally ran out in 1847 it was not renewed.

Amazingly, over 150 years after the last race a well worn path corresponding to the route of the course can still just be discerned in the northern part of the site (*see* p135), while the base of what is thought to be a marshall's box has been recently uncovered. The grassy heights are also worth visiting if only for the views.

Before leaving the Moor, one other small piece of sporting history should be noted.

In 1818, William Mitchell, a cotton spinner, established on Kersal Moor the **Manchester Golf Club**, often cited as only the second golf club formed in England (after Blackheath, 1766).

A portrait of the club's first captain and president, George Fraser, also dated 1818, hangs in Manchester City Art Gallery, and suggests that, in common with the archers of the day, a special uniform was worn.

The golf club disbanded in the 1880s, reconstituted in 1891 and subsequently changed its name to the **Old Manchester Golf Club**. Its second course on Kersal Vale (5) had nine holes and from 1891-1960 was based in a converted house on Vine Street. It is still possible to make out some of the former greens, between Vine Street and Castle Hill viewpoint.

Returning to horseracing, after Kersal Moor the Race Committee turned its attention to an area immediately to the south, overlooked by the golf course. This new location, rented for £500 per annum on a 20 year lease, was named **Castle Irwell** (6), after a mansion belonging to the owner of the site, John Fitzgerald, who also owned a colliery in Pendleton.

▲ The winding waters of the Irwell enclose the distinctive site of the former **Castle Irwell** racecourse (6), and in doing so show why much of the low lying land has been left undeveloped. Hence the Irwell Valley sporting cluster. It is also plain to see why the going at racecourse was so often soft.

In the foreground, above the weir are the pristine pitches of the **Manchester United Academy** (11). United also own **The Cliff** (16), the smaller of the two sports grounds seen bordering the far bank of the Irwell. The light roof of United's indoor training hall can

be seen clearly in the centre of the photograph. On the right edge of the photograph is the **Yew Street** cricket and rugby ground (18).

Just below this is the light roof of the racecourse's surviving **Members Stand** (7), now a student union serving the halls of residence in the south eastern corner of the site.

Also visible is the racecourse's boundary wall, in the lower right hand corner, where Cromwell Road and Littleton Road meet at the roundabout. A faded racecourse noticeboard (*right*) is still visible on this corner, over 40 years after the last race was run.

Castle Irwell was a notoriously misty, boggy and heavy-going course, for obvious reasons. But it was far more convenient and easier to manage than Kersal Moor. At the southern end, near Cromwell Road, a grandstand was built accommodating 1,000 spectators on three viewing levels, and from this, and from several other vantage points (Castle Hill, in particular), one could easily follow every race.

But still racing could not escape its negative image.

Manchester in the 1840s was ridden with petty crime, as huge numbers of transient poor arrived to seek work in the new industrial powerhouse. Meanwhile, the memory of Peterloo was still fresh enough in people's minds to make any large gathering in Manchester a potentially worrisome event.

Said one observer at Castle Irwell in 1867, 'You could not collect so many people together in favour of reform to save your life... Racing, whether for good or bad, is the most popular sport we have.'

Another visitor described the scene as 'a complete canvas city of public houses'.

John Fitzgerald's son, also John, was having none of it. After inheriting his father's estate he refused absolutely to renew the Race Committee's lease when it expired in 1867, 'for just and Christian reasons'.

Once again, a new home had to be found.

Manchester's third major race-course was at New Barns, just north of the Trafford Park estate. (*see p23, map ref. 6*). Also notoriously damp – even compared with Castle Irwell – New Barns was never popular, however, and when the land was needed for the Ship Canal's Number 9 Dock (now Salford Quays), the Race Committee grabbed the chance to return to Castle Irwell.

Only this time they went back as the owners, having bought the 132 acre site in 1898 from the executors of the very same John Fitzgerald who had evicted them 31 years previously.

With security of tenure for the first time in over 200 years, the Committee formed a company and set about turning Castle Irwell into the most advanced sports facility yet seen in Manchester.

Firstly it was enclosed entirely by stout perimeter walls, and by the curve of the river, and was thus easier to police. There were trams to the door, gardens and glazed galleries inside. This was racing for respectable folks, and for every other class of punter too. For the members, in particular, the Club Stand was especially grand.

The Castle Irwell course that was finally inaugurated on the Easter weekend of March 1902 was therefore quite different from its mid-19th century forerunner. Indeed it was, in every sense, the first purpose-built 20th century sports venue in Manchester.

From a racing perspective, its three separate tracks – flat, hurdle and steeplechase – were challenging for both jockeys and mounts. Not only was the going often heavy, despite an extensive system of drainage, but tight bends at both ends of the elongated site made for stout hearts and firm grips. Fog and mist from the Irwell added to the course's distinctive micro-climate.

But there were compensating factors. Castle Irwell was close to the city centre, and therefore top jockeys, owners and trainers were able to stay in town (the Midland Hotel being their favourite). »

Castle Irwell's original entrance building (8) on Cromwell Road, pictured in 1908 (*top*) and in 2004 (*above*), without its original Dutch gables. The block now forms a gateway to the University of Salford's Castle Irwell Student Village. The boarded up arches on the right housed turnstile entrances, while visible behind the taxi are the former ticket windows. Student facilities, including a laundrette, are incorporated into the rear of the building.

▶ Seen here shortly before its demolition in the early 1960s, the Club Stand at **Castle Irwell** racecourse, built in 1902, was an eccentric amalgam of styles. By contrast, its successor (*map ref 7*), shown below, opened in 1961, was a study in modern minimalism.

It also turned out to be one of Manchester's, and indeed Britain's oddest sporting curiosities.

Designed by Ernest Atherden, a young local architect who had recently studied the venues designed for the 1960 Rome Olympics, the structure was one of the first fully cantilevered, reinforced concrete stands built in post-war Britain (though they had been common on the Continent since the 1920s).

More significantly it was also the first stand in Britain to feature private viewing boxes, located at the rear of the open terrace.

When Atherden was subsequently commissioned to design a new stand for Manchester United, in 1964, he brought the United directors to see the Castle Irwell stand and, not without difficulty, persuaded them that they too should incorporate boxes into the new Old Trafford.

Thus was born a new form of corporate entertainment.

'Executive boxes' subsequently became standard at most football and cricket grounds, and racecourses, from the 1970s onwards, while Atherden's practice (now called Atherden Fuller Leng) went on to redesign the whole of Old Trafford, not once but twice between 1964 and 2004, as well as Liverpool's Anfield, plus several other football stands in the north west and London.

Not one of the company's designs would share the fate of the Castle Irwell stand, however.

Within barely two years of its completion, racing came to an abrupt halt at Castle Irwell, and for several years the stand lay empty; a modern folly in the eyes of those who had never warmed to its functional appearance.

Finally, when the developers who bought the racecourse were forced to abandon their plans, the stand was converted into a student union.

Staff working there today joke about a jockey's ghost, heard echoing around the building on certain nights.

And who can blame them?

Exposed and detached, in a city with a racing traditon that goes back to the 17th century, the Castle Irwell stand is a haunting and poignant reminder of what has been lost.

≫ When the November Handicap was held, the crowds spread right into the heart of the city.

The course staged England's first ever evening meeting, in July 1951. The following June at Castle Irwell, Queen Elizabeth celebrated her first winner as a race horse owner after acceding to the throne.

But as the post-war boom petered out, Castle Irwell's location started to tell. In 1961 a huge hole appeared by the winning post. A sewer shaft had collapsed. Then the Club Stand was found to be riddled with rot.

Building its replacement put a huge strain on the course's already creaking finances. So much so that within a mere two years of its opening, Castle Irwell's dispirited shareholders were persuaded to sell out to property developers.

The stand they left behind (*map ref. 7, see also left*), thus became an almost instant folly.

Castle Irwell's final race, watched by just over 20,000 spectators and aptly named the Goodbye Consolation Plate, was won by Lester Piggott, on 9 November 1963.

There have been no race meetings in the city of Manchester since that day – the longest hiatus since racing began in 1647.

As it transpired, the course's new owners failed to obtain consent for their redevelopment scheme after a public enquiry. Instead, the area where the stands and racecourse building were concentrated was developed as a student village for Salford College of Technology (now the University of Salford), while the course itself remained as open space, having been converted into pitches.

We now turn to the southern part of the Irwell Valley cluster, and perhaps the most significant site associated with cricket in the area – the tongue of land lying between the Irwell's winding waters, below The Crescent.

Referred to as the **Adelphi** (12) and still used by the University of Salford, this low-lying, self-contained ground was home, *inter alia*, to two of the earliest known cricket clubs in the area, and might therefore be considered as the cradle of Manchester cricket.

First to play there, at some time between 1818-23, was the **Aurora Cricket Club**, so-called because their games started at dawn. This club evolved into the Manchester Cricket Club, which still later evolved into the Lancashire County Cricket Club at Old Trafford.

Second was the **Broughton Cricket Club**, formed in 1823, who moved to Yew Tree Lane, now Yew Street in 1851 (18, *see* p42).

Opposite the Adelphi is the **David Lewis Recreation ground** (14). Lewis (1822-85), the founder of Lewis's Department Store, left his fortune for the benefit of the people of Manchester and Liverpool. Salford Corporation laid out the fields in c.1897, and they have been well used since.

Finally south of this lies **Peel Park** (13), another historic site hidden in the dip below the Crescent, and so, almost like a secret garden, known only to the few. Walking along Wallness Lane, it is hard to imagine that one is in the midst of a large metropolis.

Peel Park, named after Sir Robert Peel (who donated £1,000 towards its creation), was one of three Manchester parks laid out in 1846 following the 'Parks for the Citizens of Manchester Campaign' promoted by the Manchester MP, Mark Philips. Over the years two bowling greens and tennis courts were provided, but none survive.

Which to an extent sums up the curious air of detachment that characterises the Irwell Valley, at least for visitors. The bowling greens at Peel Park, set aside. The Kersal pub, demolished. Agecroft Rowing Club, relocated. Broughton Rangers, defunct. Broughton Park, gone to Hough End. Manchester Football Club, gone to Cheadle. And that is

before we mention Manchester United's part-relocation from **The Cliff** (16, *see also* p43).

Such is the ebb and flow of urban life. And yet there are still, thankfully, too many fine open spaces for this fascinating cluster to be written off yet.

'Play on Irwell Valley!' must therefore be the cry. History is on your side.

The racecourse may have long gone but the Racecourse Hotel (*10*) lives on. A Tudorbethan design with stained glass windows in racing colours, it opened in 1930. Jockeys would overnight there, perhaps dreaming of seeing their name on one of the hotel's honours boards, where winners of both the Manchester Cup from 1816-63, and the November Handicap, from 1876-1963, are listed. Across Littleton Road is the Academy Ground of Manchester United (*11*), set aside for the 9-10 year old stars of tomorrow.

The Salford Greyhound Stadium (*map ref. 9*), above in 1936 and right in the 1970s, was the least developed of the three tracks built in Manchester during the pre-war boom in greyhound racing. Opened in April 1928, a month before White City's greyhound stadium, Salford staged speedway racing, briefly, in 1928-29, and stock car racing during the 1970s, when it was also known as the Salford Albion Stadium. After it closed in 1976, a housing estate was built on most of the site, its streets being named Greyhound Drive, Basset Avenue, Collie Avenue... and so on. The Cromwell Road end is now the location of the Stanley Albion Casino. Only one greyhound stadium still operates in the Manchester are, at Belle Vue (*see Chapter 4*).

▲ Established in 1851 as the home of the **Broughton Cricket Club** (itself formed at the Adelphi in 1823), the **Yew Street cricket ground** (*18*) was for a few decades a rival to Old Trafford as the focal point for Lancashire cricket. One of Broughton's advantages was said to be the club's non-hierarchical atmosphere, in contrast to the prevailing social distinctions that persisted at Old Trafford under the patronage of the de Traffords.

WG Grace was a regular visitor to Yew Street, once hitting a ball as far as **Albert Park** (*19*). A bowls section form in the 1860s, followed by lacrosse in 1875.

On October 29 1878, a mere 15 days after the word's first ever floodlit football match at Bramall Lane, Sheffield, the Broughton area staged Manchester's first ever floodlit sports event, a rugby match between Broughton FC and a select XV from Swinton. It is unclear from reports as to whether the venue was Yew Street or The Cliff (*see opposite*). Whichever, two lights powered by Gramme dynamos, each hung from a 30 foot pole, provided intermittent illumination, watched by an estimated crowd of 10-20,000 spectators gathered in the ground and in the surrounding houses and streets. Although clearly brighter than gas lamps, the reporter from the *Salford Weekly Chronicle* did not foresee electric lights catching on.

Another first followed in July 1880 when Yew Street hosted the inaugural **Northern Tennis Tournament**. Moor Lane staged the 1881 event, before it moved to Old Trafford and, in 1908, to its current home in Didsbury.

After purchasing Yew Street from the Clowes Estate in the 1920s, Broughton CC added sections for hockey and tennis, and after 1945, rugby union. But as members moved further out to the suburbs and debts rose, part of the ground was sold for housing, and the Victorian pavilion (*above*) was replaced by a modern block with squash courts. Yew Street is now mainly known as the home of **Broughton Rugby Union FC**.

▶ Known formerly as Cliff Point, **The Cliff** sports ground (*16*), Lower Broughton Road has enjoyed a surprisingly varied sporting life.

Originally owned by the Clowes Estate and stretching uninterrupted from Higher Broughton to Cromwell Bridge, the ground's first recorded sporting tenant, c.1869, was a rugby club, **Broughton FC**, not to be confused with Broughton RUFC (*see opposite*), Broughton Rangers (*see below*), or Broughton Park RUFC (now based at Hough End).

Around the time that Broughton FC disbanded in 1898, Cliff Point was split into two by the laying out of Hugh Oldham Drive. This was named after the founder of **Manchester Grammar School**, which purchased the southern half of Cliff Point for use as its playing fields in 1899. These fields were subsequently sold on to Salford City Council in 1934 (when MGS moved to Rusholme) and have remained in use by local schools since. Of particular note is the surviving MGS pavilion, also dating from 1899, illustrated on the book's title page. It is one of the city's finest small sports buildings.

The northern section of the site was, meanwhile, leased by the **Manchester Jewish Cricket Club**, a sporting, social and literary society set up by members of Higher Broughton's growing community of Eastern European Jewish refugees, then making its mark in Manchester's cloth and garment industry. The club's aim was 'to promote athletics and out-of-door experiences generally'.

Above right is The Cliff's timber pavilion (perhaps left behind by Broughton FC), pictured on the occasion of what appears to be a Jewish wedding. The house in the background still stands, on Lower Broughton Road.

From 1913-33 The Cliff took on a wholly different character, as the home of **Broughton Rangers**.

Formed in 1877, Rangers first played on a field by Walness Bridge, where they were nicknamed 'Mrs Boardman's Boys', because the players changed at the Bridge Inn, Lower Broughton Road, run by an Isabella Boardman.

From 1892-1913 Rangers rented **Wheater's Field** (*15*), where despite a poor pitch and cramped stands, the club became founder members of the Northern Union (now Rugby League) and one of its most successful sides. Wheater's Crescent now occupies the site.

Some Rangers fans grumbled that The Cliff was at the smart end of Broughton. But for the club it was a welcome chance to expand.

Even so, viewing the site today it seems unthinkable that during Rangers' tenancy The Cliff held 26,471 spectators for a Lancashire Cup Final, in November 1931. This was a month after the photograph on the right was taken, during a league match v. Wigan. Shortly after the final, fire destroyed the club's stand (seen on the right), and with crowds dropping and debts mounting, in 1933 Rangers decamped to Belle Vue (*see p44*).

Next up was football, and football of the highest order.

For in 1938 The Cliff became the main training ground for **Manchester United**, the place where Matt Busby would nurture his 'Busby Babes' – Duncan Edwards and Bobby Charlton included – and where in later years the likes of Best, Beckham, Giggs and Scholes would learn their craft. Every training day The Cliff's car park would fill with autograph hunters and reporters, a curious invasion of this otherwise quiet suburb.

In 1999 United moved their senior training operation to Carrington, closer to where their millionaire players reside. But the club continues to use The Cliff for junior matches and community initiatives. A sports hall occupies one end, and as shown (*right*), United's 1960s administration block occupies the touchline where Rangers' main stand once stood. A terrace cover from the Rangers era also survives on the riverside.

All in all, these historical vignettes typify the sporting heritage of the Irwell Valley. Taken on their own they seem not so significant. Considered as a whole they tell quite a story.

Chapter Four

Belle Vue

Belle Vue was synonymous with sport throughout its life, and with boxing especially from 1929 onwards. Manchester still has a number of thriving boxing clubs, but nowhere is there a venue for top-flight bouts as steamy or as atmospheric as was Belle Vue's King's Hall.

Our third cluster of venues is perhaps the most aptly titled of all. By its very name the 'Belle Vue' Zoological Gardens and Pleasure Grounds announced its mission to the world. It was, as the adverts trumpeted, 'the gateway to a thousand pleasures'.

Not only was this one of Britain's most popular leisure attractions, but with the exception only of London's Vauxhall Gardens (active from c. 1660-1859) Belle Vue was the most enduring, certainly in the modern era.

Before television, multiplex cinemas and out-of-town theme parks finally rendered it obsolete in the 1980s, Belle Vue stayed open for over 140 years, long outliving its rivals in west Manchester (see Chapter 2). In the amusement park business that is a remarkably long time, spanning as it does so many shifts in urban development, public taste and, not least, technological advancement.

From a Victorian boating lake to a modern water-chute; from a maze to a ten-pin bowling alley; from brass bands to Jimmy Savile at the park's Top Ten Club in the 1960s; from candlelight to gaslight to electric light to neon, a commercial venture like Belle Vue could never rest on its laurels.

And if its pragmatic architectural style lacked the exuberance of, say, Coney Island's Luna Park, or the scale of London's Alexandra Palace, its role in the social and recreational lives of millions of people in the north west cannot be underestimated.

Above all, Belle Vue was a centre for activity, for involvement in *live* events. Time and again older Mancunians recall its buzz. Here was a place where young and old could let off steam at in a relatively controlled environment.

Of course for most of its life Belle Vue's core was its zoo, and especially its celebrated elephants. But there were other favourites; a scenic railway, Madame Tussaud's, and most prominent of all on the Gorton skyline, the 'Bobs' roller coaster, installed in 1929. ('Bobs' was a name registered by its American designer, Fred Church, to describe the roller-coaster's action, rather than because it cost a bob to ride, as is often thought.)

But what of sport?

With the aid of various histories of the park (see page 130) and the company's archives held at Chetham's Library, we revisit Belle Vue here for two reasons.

Firstly, Belle Vue was a hub of sporting activity throughout most of its years in business. Indeed sport lent Belle Vue a diversity that no other British amusement park could rival, apart only from Crystal Palace during its Sydenham days, from 1864-1936.

Secondly, the one single element of the complex that has survived – the greyhound stadium on Kirkmanshulme Lane – also happens to be an important part of Britain's sporting heritage; not for architectural reasons but because it was the first dog track ever built outside the United States.

In order to understand why and how that came about we must thus consider Belle Vue not as it is now – as a single venue – but as the cluster of venues it once formed.

The story begins in the 1820s at the Belle Vue House inn, on the recently opened turnpike road between Manchester and Hyde.

The inn, built in 1819, lay close to where the Showcase Cinema now stands on Hyde Road. Set in spacious grounds, it offered a tea garden, a small menagerie at the rear, and a bowling green.

The first individual to realise the site's potential was John Jennison, a gardener, who took on the lease in 1837 and whose family would manage and develop Belle Vue for the next 88 years. Sport would form a vital arm of the Jennisons' business, as it would at most pleasure gardens of the period.

This was, nevertheless, a precarious business. Many Victorian parks lasted only a few years and bankruptcies were common. Jennison himself only just survived lean times in the early 1840s, and, although we cannot be certain of the linkage, it is interesting to note that two contemporaries of Belle Vue, the Manchester Zoological Gardens at Higher Broughton and Vauxhall Gardens in Collyhurst, did not promote sport, as did Belle Vue, and neither survived.

One of Belle Vue's earliest sporting attractions was **coursing**, a longstanding rural tradition in which dogs are set loose in pursuit of a rabbit or hare, while onlookers bet on the winner.

Unfortunately for Jennison the police banned it in 1842, not to prevent cruelty to animals but because it attracted unruly crowds. This was a time of social unease and petty crime in Manchester, and the authorities were taking no chances. But the very fact that coursing was so popular in the area would have ramifications several decades later.

Less controversially, Jennison also laid out a sports field for **cricket** and **archery** at the western edge of the site (bordered by what

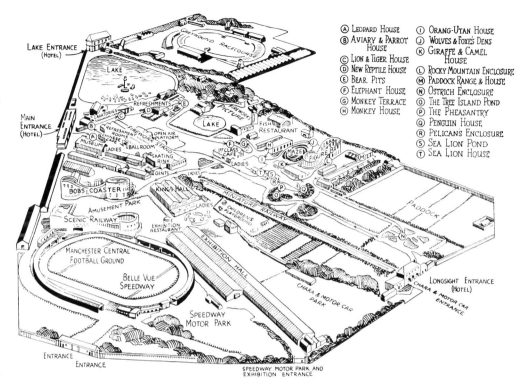

are now Pottery and Redgate Lanes). The grounds were also used over the years for **foot races**.

In fact pedestrianism, or athletics as it became known, would turn out to be Belle Vue's first established spectator sport. This began in 1887 when Jennison's sons, who had by now inherited the business, laid out a permanent athletics track with stands on part of the Belle Vue sports field closest to Hyde Road.

Whether a coincidence or not, a similar enclosure was constructed that same year at the Botanical Gardens in Old Trafford, as part of the Jubilee Exhibition grounds.

Old Trafford's track was sponsored by the city's amateur athletic elite, under the auspices of the Manchester Athletics Club.

Belle Vue's track, meanwhile, became the main home of **Salford Harriers**. Formed by cross country champion Harry Hardwick in 1884, Salford was a different breed of club; commercially minded, fiercely competitive, and quick to sign up some of the nation's top athletes, including Olympic gold medallist Alfred Tysoe and WH 'Sonny' Morton, who beat the Irish-American champion, TP Connell, at Belle Vue in 1891. Crowds of 10,000 for such events were common, and the profits were considerable.

Another large crowd at Belle Vue, estimated at 12,000, attended a floodlit football match, played between Ardwick (now Manchester City) and Newton Heath (Manchester United), in »

Belle Vue as it appeared in the 1931 Guide Book. Not a single structure from the main complex survives in situ, leaving only the 'greyhound racecourse' on the opposite side of Kirkmanshulme Lane to carry on the Belle Vue name. The stadium is now shared with the Belle Vue Aces speedway team, since the demolition of the speedway stadium in 1987. Note also the small lake, used in winter for skating and curling, and the roller skating rink, added during a renewed bout of 'rincomania' in Britain in 1910 (see Chapter 13). Opposite the rink was the King's Hall, also built in 1910 and for many years Manchester's top boxing venue.

ISSUED EVERY SATURDAY

The Belle Vue Aces were the dominant speedway club of the 1930s, sometimes drawing crowds of over 30,000 to their purpose-built stadium on Hyde Road (see right). Even during the 1970s, when the Aces fielded local hero Peter Collins, crowds of 15,000 were still common. Now they register around a tenth of that. One of the great attractions of attending speedway meetings at Belle Vue, particularly for visiting fans from out of town, was that entry to the stadium also allowed you entry into the amusement park, thus providing an action-packed Saturday night's entertainment.

》 February 1889. Staged with the aid of 20 Well's Lights and kicked off by Charles Jennison, the match raised £140 for the victims of a colliery disaster at nearby Hyde.

Other sporting activities offered at Belle Vue were **ice skating**, on the frozen lake (1847 onwards), **rowing** (1875), **tennis** and **croquet** (1877) – the Jennisons were great ones for attending Wimbledon – **curling** (1890s), and **roller skating** (1910).

In John Jennison's days Belle Vue also experimented with **horse racing**, in 1847, and with a small **swimming pool** added in the early 1850s, before the city had its own first baths (see Chapter 17). Neither was a success.

By the end of World War One Belle Vue was nearly a century old and was a much loved part of Manchester life. But in 1920 the Jennisons were presented with an opportunity that might well have changed the course, not only of Belle Vue's development, but of Manchester football too.

Manchester City had been neighbours of Belle Vue since their formative years in the early 1880s. In fact all three of City's earliest grounds bordered the park, and had the Jennisons spotted the potential of this emerging sport on their doorstep they might well have offered the club a berth.

In 1920 a fire destroyed the main stand at City's Hyde Road ground, a short distance from Belle Vue. This setback, and the inadequacies of the ground in general, forced City to consider a new home.

Belle Vue seemed the obvious choice. It was on a main road, with two stations close at hand, and it lay in the heart of City's traditional fan base.

But the Jennisons were only prepared to offer a 50 year lease, and the athletics ground site was relatively small, at only eight acres (although there was space to expand). So, after two years' deliberation, and to the surprise of the *Manchester Evening News* at any rate, City's directors dropped Belle Vue and opted for Maine Road, even though it was in a completely different area of the city.

Now of course City are back in east Manchester, after the closure of Maine Road in 2003.

Belle Vue still needed a fresh injection of life, however. Its attractions were looking tired. Fashions had moved on. This was the age of cinema, of electricity, of aeroplanes and the wireless. Belle Vue needed a modern man, and in John Henry Iles they found him.

Iles was steeped in the leisure business. In 1919 he had helped design Margate's Dreamland complex. He had also worked on various fairgrounds around Europe and Buenos Aires. Most impressively, he had just managed the amusement park at the 1924 Empire Exhibition at Wembley.

Oddly enough, Maine Road, which opened in the same year as the new Wembley Stadium, 1923, was often called the Wembley of the North. But Belle Vue had the more tangible claim, because when Iles' newly formed management company took over Belle Vue from the Jennisons in 1925, one of his first coups was to arrange for several rides from the Wembley exhibition to be re-erected at Belle Vue, after the London exhibition closed.

To these Iles added the Scenic Railway in 1928 – 'it puts the wind up you, through you and round you' – and the Bobs, in 1929. 'If you can ride the Bobs you're good for a 100!'

But Iles' most lasting contribution, in sporting terms at least, was to be party to the introduction of first, greyhound racing from the United States in 1926 (see p50) and, two years later, speedway, from Australia.

Speedway was a thoroughly modern construct. Like dog racing it was staged at night, under lights (while the football authorities remained resolutely opposed to

floodlit matches). Its buccaneering helmeted riders, leather-clad and wearing steel tipped boots, were like speed jockeys of the new mechanical age. It was noisy, fast, and at times dangerous too.

Speedway's first official outing in Britain was in Essex in February 1928. But Manchester was close behind, staging its first meeting at the Snipe Trotting Track, Audenshaw, three weeks later. Several of London's greyhound stadiums snapped up licenses soon after, followed by White City in Old Trafford, in June 1928.

Iles was on the case straight away. After trials on the grass infield of the greyhound stadium, by July 1928 he had laid a proper cinder track and, in the process, made sure White City would not gain the upper hand.

Elsewhere in Britain over 60 other tracks were hastily prepared.

The public was entranced.

As, clearly, was Iles. For whilst other speedway promoters were content to double up at greyhound stadiums – all of them virtually brand new – Iles insisted on

a completely new stadium for speedway, on the site of Belle Vue's athletics ground.

With a capacity of 34,000, including 20,000 seats (a large proportion for the time, suggesting that Iles was aiming upmarket), this new venue (*shown above*) opened on March 23 1929.

Like most greyhound and speedway stadiums of the period, it was, nevertheless, a hurriedly built, utilitarian venue which would not wear well or stand up to modern scrutiny. But in the speedway world it was a relative palace, ranked second only to London's White City Stadium, built for the 1908 Olympics.

Unsurprisingly, speedway's bright promise soon fizzled, with teams and tracks going out of business almost as quickly as they had emerged. But the Aces at least lived up to their name by winning more honours than any other club during the 1930s.

The indefatigable Iles, meanwhile, was keen to fill his new stadium as often as possible. Thus he formed a football club, »

Since the loss of the speedway stadium in 1987, the Belle Vue Aces have raced at the greyhound stadium, where the shale speedway track lies on the inside of the sand covered dog track, an arrangement common to many shared stadiums. There are currently around 40 speedway clubs in Britain. A typical match consists of 15-20 heats, each of which sees four riders complete four laps. This typically takes 60 seconds. Speedway bikes, incidentally, have one handlebar longer than the other, and despite being capable of speeds of up to 120mph, possess no gears, no suspension, and no brakes. The smell of their burning oil, it is said by afficionados, can be quite addictive.

▲ Manchester's boxing scene was at its peak when JH Iles revamped Belle Vue's **King's Hall** as a 6,000 seat arena in the late 1920s.

The city was at this time awash with small halls and boxing booths, known graphically as 'blood tubs'; the Adelphi Sporting Club and the Flat Iron, both in Salford, the Junction Stadium on Oldham Road, and the Alhambra, Openshaw. The Free Trade Hall was another popular venue, as was the Winter Gardens on Peter Street.

For most of the 1930s the main draw was a trio of local fighters known as the 'Three Cavaliers', some of whose more illustrious bouts were switched to Belle Vue's speedway stadium (see previous page), where they were watched by crowds of up to 30,000.

Trained at the Collyhurst & Moston Lads' Club, the Cavaliers were Jackie Brown, a fast living

boy from Collyhurst who beat the Tunisian, Victor 'Young' Perez, at Belle Vue in 1932 to become world flyweight champion; Johnny King, the bantamweight champion from 1935-47, and hard-hitting middleweight Joe Bamford, the 'Rochdale Thunderbolt', who fought under the name Jock McAvoy because he did not want his mother to know what he was up to.

Another favourite was Clayton born middleweight Len Johnson, barred from championship fights by the British Boxing Board of Control because he was black. After retiring from the ring Johnson became a Communist activist in the city. Also on the Belle Vue bill during the 1930s was wrestling, put on by Kathleen Lock, Britain's only female wrestling promoter.

Always atmospheric but never regal, the King's Hall was finally demolished in 1982.

» Manchester Central, and, as a publicity stunt, appointed as its coach one of the city's greatest ever football luminaries, the Welsh international, Billy Meredith.

Meredith, who had played for both United and City before retiring in 1924, at the ripe old age of 50, was running the Stretford Road Hotel at the time.

But even with Meredith's involvement, Central failed to gain a following – as do most artificially created football entities – and the club disbanded in 1932.

Never one to give in, Iles turned next to rugby league.

Broughton Rangers, based at the Cliff, Salford (see p43), had fallen on hard times, and were thus easily lured to Belle Vue with an offer of £4,000. But again, after years of struggle and despite a change of name to Belle Vue Rangers, the club folded in 1955.

Rather more successful was the introduction of stock car racing in 1954, complete with an American-style troupe known as 'Johnnie's Marching Girls'. Johnnie Hoskins, a charismatic New Zealander who had been among the early pioneers of speedway, was then promoter of the Belle Vue Aces.

In common with all amusement parks and sports venues, Belle Vue experienced an extraordinary boom during the post war years. On the Easter weekend of 1946, a record 250,000 visitors passed through the turnstiles.

But thereafter decline beckoned. In 1963 Charles Forte purchased the whole park apart from the greyhound stadium – which remained in the hands of the Greyhound Racing Association – and on the site of the lake built a ten-pin bowling alley (itself now demolished). But the downward

trend proved irreversible. In 1971 the Bobs was demolished. The zoo closed in 1977 and in 1982 the King's Hall put on its final circus.

That same year the Hyde Road speedway stadium was sold to a speedway and stock car racing promoter, who tidied it up and tried various novelty events, such as American football, but then finally closed it down after new safety legislation following the Bradford fire of 1985 finally exposed its frailties.

Much to the ire of Aces fans, the site was redeveloped by the British Car Auction group in 1988.

Other than a few momentoes in the auction building, all traces of the stadium have otherwise gone, (although there is a Hoskins Close, and a Lockhart Close, named after George Lockhart, Belle Vue's long serving ringmaster, on the neighbouring estate.)

But before growing too maudlin, it could be argued that there are modern versions of Belle Vue elsewhere in Manchester, at the Trafford Centre, say, or even the Print Works. And that in time, no doubt, these too will be sold off to make way for the next 'big thing' in the leisure world. As Messrs Jennison and Iles would readily concede, that's showbiz.

Yet which bits of Belle Vue's legacy live on? Why, those two fads of the late 1920s, greyhounds and speedway. And what do we now find next door to the greyhound track? A £3.2 million centre for hockey and cricket, constructed for the Commonwealth Games.

So there is still sport at Belle Vue, as well as a multiplex cinema, and although together these may not add up to 'a thousand pleasures', the Belle Vue name lives on, and may yet rise again.

◄ Greyhound racing made its debut in Britain at Belle Vue in July 1926. But why Belle Vue?

As already mentioned, rabbit coursing had been a feature at Belle Vue in the early 19th century. Coursing was, and remains (however controversially) one of the simplest of countryside sports. In essence, two greyhounds are unleashed to chase after a hare on open ground, while spectators bet on the winner. Often the prey escapes, but it is still no sport for the sensitive (though in the 18th and 19th centuries it was less gory than bear baiting or cockfighting).

Britain's first coursing club, which still exists, was formed at Swaffham, Norfolk, in 1776. By 1850 there were over 380 others, with the Waterloo Cup held at Altcar, Liverpool, said to attract crowds of up to 75,000. (It was organised from 1836 onwards in tandem with the Grand National at Aintree.) One year, so legend has it, the London Stock Exchange closed early when news of the Waterloo winner arrived by carrier pigeon.

A major problem for coursing was that it was hard for large crowds to follow the action.

One solution, tried at the Welsh Harp, Hendon, in 1876, was a mechanical hare moving on a rail. But the straight course was not felt to be a true test of the dogs' skills and it was not tried again.

However in the United States an entrepreneur called Owen P Smith finally found the answer in 1912. Anxious to stem criticism of coursing from animal rights campaigners, he experimented with various types of mechanical hare. But his cleverest idea was also the most obvious, and that was to turn the straight course into a loop, like an athletics track, thereby allowing more spectators to watch.

Ironically, Smith opposed gambling, and it would be several years before he gave in to demands for bookmakers to attend his tracks, some time in the mid 1920s. But once that happened, the traps flew open all over the United States.

Knowing of the British love of coursing and of gambling, another American businessman, Charles Munn, tried for months to find backers in Britain – not easy with a General Strike looming – but two investors, Brigadier-General Alfred Critchley and Sir William Gentle eventually raised £22,000 and formed the Greyhound Racing Association.

It was this pair who saw Belle Vue, with its coursing tradition, its new dynamic manager, JH Iles, and its famous name, as the ideal place to start.

Belle Vue's £20,000 new track, noted *Country Life* on the eve of the stadium's opening on July 24 1926, could accommodate 25,000 spectators, including 2,000 in a covered stand. (That same stand survives today, albeit much altered, as can be seen on the right)

Perhaps not wishing to give too much credit to the Americans, *Country Life* went on to describe how the Belle Vue track was set up.

'The racecourse, as we have known it for so long in this country, is, frankly, the model on which the greyhound track is designed. There is a paddock for the parade; there are the scales for "weighing in"; there are stables and trainers and kennel-boys. It is just horse-racing over again, except that the greyhound runs without whip or spur and has to carry his own silk.'

The 'hare', it added, was capable of 55 miles per hour.

Whether any readers of *Country Life* considered this new sport worthy of attending we shall never

know, but only 1700 spectators turned up at the opening, on July 24 1926. A striking miner from Newton Heath called Johnny Jones blew a bugle to signal the first race, and a red dog in a blue jacket called Mistley took the honour (at odds of 6-1) in just 25 seconds. Fifty years later the main stand was named after him.

After the poorly attended debut, crowds soon picked up, and by 1939 Britain had over a hundred tracks. In 1946 attendances totalled a staggering 34 million (compared with 35.6 million for football). Since then numbers have plummeted, but although many predicted the sport would die, it has revived in recent years and now attracts just under four million spectators annually at some 50 venues.

▲ Belle Vue is Manchester's sole remaining greyhound stadium, following the closure of White City and Salford. As is the norm nowadays, spectators gather in one stand, many preferring to congregate in the glass-fronted lounge inserted into the rake of the original stand (*shown opposite in 1926, top, and 2002, below*).

Apart from the paddock in front of this stand, the terraces around the rest of the track are unused.

Greyhound stadiums are, without exception, functional in design, with few concessions to architectural style.

On the other hand, greyhound goers are also noted for their almost total lack of pretension. General admission to Belle Vue is £5-6. Betting stakes are as low as 50 pence, and although the form

guides are fearsomely hard for novices to follow, as are the various modes of betting – trifecta, anyone? – there are always helpful punters on hand to proffer advice. Indeed Belle Vue is undergoing something of a revival these days, drawing around 6,000 punters a week.

Nowadays all of them pass through the main doors of the stand, thereby missing out what is Belle Vue's only architectural feature of any note; its early 1960s, gull-winged turnstile block, now disused and concealed behind hoardings. Yet as the photograph on page 69 shows, if tidied up and suitably lit, given its location on the busy junction of Hyde Road and Mount Road, it could form an eye-catching marker for the stadium, as well as providing a token reminder of Belle Vue's racier days.

Chapter Five

Sportcity

OPPOSITE THIS PLAQUE WAS THE
BANK STREET GROUND
HOME OF
MANCHESTER UNITED
FORMERLY NEWTON HEATH F.C.
1893 TO 1910

Four miles currently separate Manchester's Blues from its Reds, but for seventeen years the clubs were near neighbours. City were based on Bennett Street, off Hyde Road, Ardwick, from 1887-1923, while from 1893-1910 United's home was Bank Street, Clayton. This plaque is on a house opposite the site, which now serves as a car park for the National Cycling Centre, one of five sports venues within the Sportcity complex.

Manchester's fourth sporting cluster – the main focal point of the 2002 Commonwealth Games – is its most modern, in both form and concept.

Branded 'Sportcity', it is a rare British example of a large scale, pre-planned stadium and multi-sport complex, brought into being by sheer political will and funded predominantly by the public purse.

Such complexes are common overseas. But in Britain only a few have ever existed, most notably at Crystal Palace, London, Meadowbank, Edinburgh (built for the 1974 Commwealth Games) and Don Valley, Sheffield (host of the 1991 World Student Games). All three, however, are on a much smaller scale than Sportcity.

(Wembley does not fall into the same category as its stadium and arena are privately owned and hired out for specific events rather than run as year-round centres for sports development.)

Sportcity is significant for other reasons too. At 146 hectares it is Britain's largest brownfield site to have been regenerated using sport as the catalyst.

It is also Britain's first publicly funded sport complex to house a senior football club. Not only does this generate thousands of users and visitors to the the complex on a regular basis, but Sportcity also gains from the high media profile that, with respect to other sports, only Premiership football can deliver.

But perhaps most importantly of all, Sportcity is a prime example of how the staging of an event such as the Commonwealth or Olympic Games can provide a lasting legacy for a host city and its people, and thereby go some way towards justifying the significant sums of public funds invested; £135 million in Manchester's case for the sports venues alone, plus several more major grants for reclamation and regeneration projects around the area.

All over the world can be found grandiose stadiums and sports complexes that once held the world's attention, only for them to gather dust after the circus has left town. Not Sportcity. The 2002 Commonwealth Games might have lasted only ten days, but its

after effects will be felt in east Manchester for decades to come. One estimate is that Sportcity will eventually be used or visited by up to 4.5 million people per year.

As a concept, Sportcity owes its origins to four separate bids made by Manchester City Council during the 1980s and 1990s.

The first, launched in 1985, was for the 1996 Olympic Games. For this bid Manchester's stadium complex was to be sited in an area close to where the Trafford Centre now stands, to the west of the city.

Atlanta won on that occasion, and by the time the City Council and its partners had launched a fresh bid for the 2000 Games, the focus had switched to a part of east Manchester known as Bradford, but rebranded thereafter as Eastlands. Blighted over the years by the closure of a coal mine, two steel plants, the Stuart Street Power Station, the Bradford Gas Works and of sundry other chemical and engineering firms, the area had become a wasteland.

Sport was to be its saviour.

The idea of using sporting facilities for regeneration

had already been successfully applied by Barcelona for the 1992 Olympics. On a lesser scale it was similarly the key to stadium developments in several British cities during the 1990s. Don Valley was the first, followed by Huddersfield, Middlesbrough, Derby and Sunderland.

Sport's potency as a magnet for regeneration was in fact one of the great discoveries of planning in post-industrial Britain.

Manchester's hopes for the 2000 Olympics were shattered when Sydney won the vote in 1993.

But such was the momentum of the city's sports development strategy – Sportcity's first venue, the National Cycling Centre was well on its way to completion by then, as was the new arena

at Victoria Station – that two parallel bids followed in 1995; to build a new national stadium at Eastlands (a competition won predictably by the incumbents, Wembley), and for this stadium to be the centrepiece for the 2002 Commonwealth Games.

With this latter bid the city was finally successful, as announced in November 1995.

This left one major hurdle to overcome, and that was to persuade Manchester City to relinquish their ground at Maine Road (*see p60*) and become tenants of the proposed stadium. Without this deal the long term viability of the stadium would have been severely at risk.

But City did sign up (*as detailed on p57*) and with some £70 millioin

of Lottery and government funding now in place to back the Games – albeit still not enough, as events transpired – Sportcity's future was at last assured.

As a new cluster it might seem there is little to say about Sportcity in the context of sporting heritage.

Yet specific events constitute in themselves an important element of how we perceive heritage. Think of the FA Cup Final at Wembley or the Grand National at Aintree. In sport, places and events are often absolutely synonymous.

The very staging of the Commonwealth Games in 2002 was therefore an event – a communal happening even – that will, without question, go down as one of the most important landmarks in the city's history.

Old meets new on Alan Turing Way, from where the City of Manchester Stadium and the National Tennis Centre (*right*) can be seen alongside the Ashton Canal. The canal, opened in 1796, once linked the heavily industrialised districts of Clayton and Openshaw with the warehouses of Ancoats. Now it offers a pedestrian walkway from Piccadilly to Sportcity. The stadium's eight distinctive masts each rise from the core of a spiral ramp. Such ramps have been commonly used for crowd circulation at north American venues since the 1970s, though this is their first appearance in Britain.

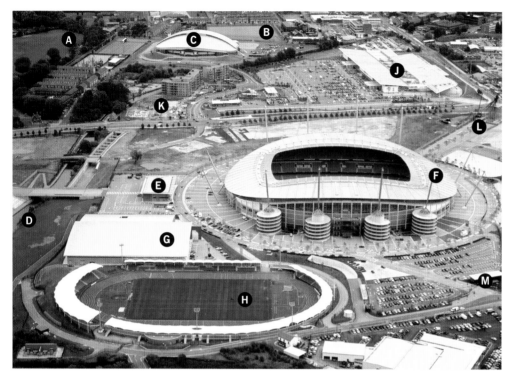

For all its modernity, the **Sportcity** area does retain some historic elements. Apart from the Ashton Canal, on Sportcity's north east flank is **Philips Park**, laid out in 1846 and with two of the city's oldest municipal bowling greens still in use, dating from 1872. The park was also the site (*marked A, above*) of the city's first open air swimming pool (*see p121*), from 1892-1949.

Sportcity also encompasses the site of Manchester United's former ground on **Bank Street** (*B*).

A 1907 match report from the *Manchester Guardian* indicates how industrialised and polluted the vicinity was at the time.

'All the time the struggle was waging, the 30 Clayton chimneys smoked and gave forth their pungent odours, and the boilers behind (one) goal poured mists of steam over the ground.'

Where those boilers were sited is now the **National Cycling Centre** (*C, and see right*), designed by the Newcastle-based architects FaulknerBrowns.

FaulknerBrowns have played a key role at Sportcity as designer of four of its five venues (plus the Aquatics Centre on Oxford Road). Together with Arup Associates, who oversaw Sportcity's masterplan and the design of the main stadium, this has ensured that although each structure has a distinct character there is a uniform palette of tones (mint green copper, grey, blue and silver), and materials (blue engineering bricks, stucco embossed facings, metallic cladding and seamed, curved profile roofing).

Also by FaulknerBrowns, on the opposite bank of the Ashton Canal, is the **Manchester Tennis Centre** (*just out of view, at D*). Opened by Tim Henman in September 2003 this has six indoor and six outdoor courts for public and schools use.

From here a pedestrian walkway, **Joe Mercer Way** (named after the much loved former Manchester City manager), crosses the canal and leads to a rectangular steel and glass block (*E*), known as **Reebok City**. This houses the Manchester City club shop, The City Social Café Bar and the club's much-praised museum, **The Manchester City Experience**.

Which leads us to Sportscity's largest, most prominent venue, the **City of Manchester Stadium** (*F*).

When opened in athletics mode for the 2002 Commonwealth Games the stadium had 38,000 seats and a temporary, open stand at the north end (close to Reebok City). As explained on p56, this stand and the track was removed after the Games, to create a seamless, 48,000 capacity football-only venue ready for the Blues in August 2003.

Facing the stadium's north west corner is a fourth venue (*G*), in two sections. The copper green roof (closest to Reebok City) marks the **National Squash Centre**, which has six courts and one moveable show court (with glass sides), plus the offices of squash's governing body, formerly based in London.

Adjoining this (in the foreground) is the larger **Indoor Athletics Centre**, where a 200m track is in regular use by the building's other occupants, the **English Institute of Sport**. One of nine regional centres which make up the Institute, the EIS's role is to train and monitor elite athletes. The track is also used by local clubs, including Sale Harriers.

Finally, in the lowest part of the site and pressed in, somewhat awkwardly, between the indoor centre and Rowsley Street, is the **Manchester Regional Arena** (*H*). Built around the warm-up track used for the 2002 Games, this was financed by a £3 million grant from the North West Development Agency. It has 6,178 seats in three sections, each covered by annular fabric awnings, and was another FaulknerBrowns design in association with TTH Architects.

Darren Campbell, the Olympic and Commonwealth Games gold medallist – originally from Moss Side – opened the arena in January 2004. The following July it staged the Norwich Union Olympic Trials, and also the AAA Championships, the first time these had been held in Manchester since 1907 (when Fallowfield was the venue).

Despite its modest scale the arena is now Manchester's prime athletics venue, as well as serving as the home ground for Manchester City's reserve team.

Sportcity is not reserved exclusively for sport, however.

This being the modern era of public/private partnerships, a substantial portion of the site is taken up by an ASDA Wal-Mart superstore (J), whilst a residential enclave (K) has been developed alongside the canal.

Meanwhile one of the newest attractions is a spectacular artwork.

In addition to Colin Spofforth's inspirational sculpture, located by the Indoor Athletics Centre (seen on p7), Sportcity is now home to Britain's tallest sculpture, **The B of the Bang** (L), by former Manchester art student Tom Heatherwick.

Installed in 2004 its name derives from the sprinter Linford Christie, who always aimed to leave the starting block, he said, on 'the b of the bang'.

Heatherwick's spikily explosive opus and its unique sporting surrounds make Sportcity one of Manchester's leading visitor attractions, which is why the management company with overall responsibility for the complex, New East Manchester Ltd., has had to set up a visitor centre in one corner of the site (M).

But as Sportcity matures – for it is still unfinished in parts and its landscaping needs to take root – the biggest challenge will not be an influx of tourists but ensuring that the site retains its sporting emphasis and is not overtaken by commercial considerations.

As we have seen with earlier sporting clusters, that is a process already familiar to Manchester.

▲ It is no fluke that Britain's performances in international cycling events – four medals at the 2004 Athens Olympics most recently – have improved markedly since the opening of the **National Cycling Centre** in September 1994.

Together with the indoor arena at Victoria Station (see p101), which opened ten months later, the velodrome's completion sent out a clear signal that Manchester meant business in its wider strategic aims.

It also revealed the City Council's new found talent for levering funds.

Of the cycling centre's £9.5m costs, £2m came from the Sports Council (now Sport England), £1m from the Foundation for Sports and Arts, and £6.5m from the Department of the Environment.

Externally the velodrome is characterised by its 122m span, twin truss roof arch and curved roof wings, which mirror the profile of the cambered track inside.

FaulknerBrowns were again the designers, working in association with the engineers Oscar Faber and the construction company AMEC, who played a lead role in the early development of Sportcity.

Internally the centre's 250m Siberian pine track – pinned down by 360,000 nails and angled 42° at its steepest – was laid by Ron Webb, a leading track designer. It has already helped produce several world records. In addition there are 3,500 seats and an in-track area used for various sports, including basketball and martial arts.

Reg Harris (1920-92) was the Stanley Matthews of the cycle track, a true British icon. He joined the Manchester Wheelers at Fallowfield in 1938 (see p62), became world amateur sprint champion in 1947, won a silver medal at the 1948 Olympics, and was world professional sprint champion four times from 1949-54. In 1974, at the age of 54, he returned to the saddle and took the British sprint title. He was twice voted BBC Sports Personality of the Year, and now his image, struck in bronze by James Butler, watches over the inviting track of the National Cycling Centre. Reg would have loved the place.

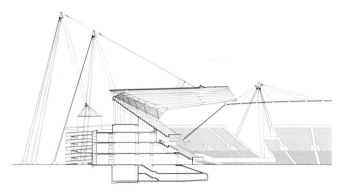
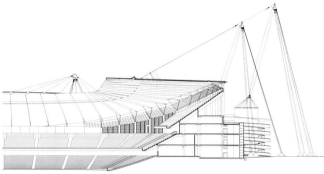

▲ One of the great conundrums of stadium design is how to reconcile the different viewing requirements of athletics and field sports.

Watching football across a running track is a common experience overseas, but is frowned upon by British fans. The action is too far away and all sense of intimacy with the players is lost.

Moreover, apart from the highest profile events, such as the Olympics, World Championships or Commonwealth Games – which come to town only once in a lifetime, if at all – it is rare for athletics meetings to attract a signifcant number of spectators.

Arup Associates' designs for the **City of Manchester Stadium** circumvented this dilemma in a highly original fashion.

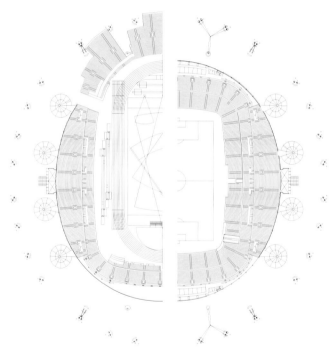

athletics mode   football mode

For the 2002 Games, three sides of the bowl on the upper tiers, and three sides of the cable net roof structure were in place, with a temporary, uncovered stand placed at the north end of the track.

Literally within hours of the Queen performing the Games' closing ceremony on August 4, the stadium contractors, Laing, started removing the temporary stand and the track, before excavating the ground level to a depth of six metres. This allowed the lower tier of seats to be extended downwards and for the upper tiers and roof to be joined up, a process which completed the bowl, raised the capacity from 38 - 48,000, and brought the front row of seats to within a few metres of the new football pitch's touchlines.

▲ From the back streets of Moss Side and the unfortunate mish-mash of stands that was Maine Road (*see p60*), to the wide-open spaces and tidy symmetry of the £110 million City of Manchester Stadium, was as great a leap as any set of British football fans has had to make since the wholesale transformation of the football landscape began in the early 1990s, in the wake of the Hillsborough disaster.

Such a culture shock might take years to dissipate before fans can call this new stadium 'home'.

Yet in one sense it might never be truly home. In Britain, unlike several of our continental neighbours, football stadiums are owned privately, by the club. It is one reason why so many develop along such haphazard lines. It is also why fans feel such a strong sense of belonging and attachment.

But at the City of Manchester Stadium, or Eastlands as some prefer, Manchester City are tenants of Manchester City Council.

As one scornful rival put it – for this has been a truly revolutionary deal in football circles – the Blues have sold their family home and moved into a council house.

Yet without City's involvement, the whole plan for Sportcity and the Commonwealth Games would have been far tougher to deliver. Both parties have therefore grabbed each other's coat-tails in a merry dance.

In simple terms, City have a 250 year lease which requires them to pay a rent based on all ticket sales over 34,000 (which was the final capacity at Maine Road).

As their average gates since moving in 2003 have been only just short of capacity, at around 47,000 (their highest averages ever, incidentally), this suggests an annual rent of £1-2 million.

The club is also responsible for the stadium's routine maintenance and upkeep.

These costs are, however, offset by a higher income than Maine Road was ever able to generate.

Based on revenue, therefore, the move has so far been a success. Based on results, City being City, as ever, erratic form appears still to be the norm...

But in design terms their new home is exemplary. As seen above, the tiers are configured in a quadric plan – that is, slightly curved along each touchline. Rarely found in Britain because of the expense, this offers the best possible sightlines for fans all round. The stadium's ramps and concourses also make for an efficient venue in terms of crowd management and circulation.

If there is a caveat it is that the stadium could be judged to be too small for City's fanbase. Nor is it designed to be easily expandable.

Only time will tell whether this becomes an issue. But for now, this is a bold and brave set up of which all parties can be proud.

Such is the bond between fans and their 'home ground' that over the years many have chosen to have their ashes scattered on the 'sacred turf'. Understandably this practice does not meet with universal approval. It can also lead to upset should a ground be sold and the club move on. At the City of Manchester Stadium, Manchester City have created a sensitive alternative in the form of a memorial garden in the stadium precincts. Also within this garden are remnants of masonry from the Hyde Hotel (demolished in 2001), where the players used to change when City moved to Hyde Road in 1887, and where City fans would traditionally gather before games. Also in the garden is a mosaic from Maine Road (*shown overleaf*).

Chapter Six

Stadiums and Grounds

Manchester City's Maine Road possessed few features worth preserving, but this mosaic – one of three located above entrances to the main stand – was saved during the ground's demolition in 2003 by mosaic artist and City fan Mark Kennedy. Designed by A & O Stefanutti & Co, of Cheetham, and installed at the time of the ground's construction in 1923 by Conway and Co, tilers of Bridge Street, the mosaic is now on display in the memorial garden at the City of Manchester stadium (*see previous page*).

There is not a major metropolis on the planet without at least one stadium. A stadium is as much a part of the urban matrix as a town hall, a public library or a concert hall. Stadiums are at the pinnacle of sport's architectural hierarchy; the most ancient in form and the most favoured as showcases by governments, politicians and sporting bodies.

In Britain the distinction between a 'stadium' and a 'ground' is a fine one, determined less by architectural parameters than by perception.

For all its scale and status, few people ever considered Manchester City's Maine Road (*see p60*) as a stadium. It was a football ground. A large one, it is true, but a ground all the same. Yet the dog track at Belle Vue, a fraction of the size of Maine Road, is known as a stadium.

Equally, Old Trafford cricket ground, which holds 19,000, would never be described as a stadium, even though it is patently a more sophisticated venue than the nearby Longford Park Stadium (*see p63*), which seats just 700.

Ultimately the distinction may be one of semantics. But the lack of definition does highlight one of the characteristics of British sports architecture which is often noted.

As mentioned earlier, the majority of our stadiums and grounds are owned privately, rather than by the public sector, as is the norm in Europe (though there are exceptions; Holland and Spain, for example). In this respect, the publicly funded City of Manchester Stadium is unique at a senior level of sport in Britain.

A consequence of private ownership is the tradition of incremental development; that is, stands have been built as and when funds have become available, using different architects at different periods. In this respect, Manchester United's Old Trafford is unique in that its development has always been tailored to a pre-designed masterplan.

For what it is worth, we may therefore conclude that a stadium is pre-planned and built in pre-determined phases, whereas a ground develops informally and on an ad-hoc basis.

Three disasters have brought about a revolution in the design and management of British stadiums and grounds.

The Ibrox disaster of 1971, in Glasgow, prompted the introduction of the 1975 Safety of Sports Grounds Act, under which all venues of a certain size have to be licensed by the local authority.

A fire in a timber stand at Valley Parade, Bradford, in 1985, led to a widening of the licensing system and to further controls on the use of timber stands and on the design of entry and exit routes.

In the Manchester area this resulted in the condemnation of individual stands at Bury's Gigg Lane, Rochdale's Spotland, and Stockport County's Edgeley Park. Two venues deemed by their owners to be beyond cost-effective restitution were Belle Vue's speedway stadium in 1987, followed by Rochdale Hornets' Athletic Grounds the year after.

Finally, the 1989 Hillsborough disaster in Sheffield led to the adoption in 1990 of a series of radical recommendations by Lord Justice Taylor.

Chief amongst these was the phasing out of standing terraces at our leading football venues.

This measure was greeted with considerable opposition. For odd as it might seem to those not familiar with the practice, standing, and the ability to mingle on a terrace, was regarded by many as an intrinsic part of the match-day experience, as a basic right even. But in any case, if terraces were unsafe for football, why were they still allowed at rugby?

Since the all-seater rule came into force in 1994, it is further argued, the atmosphere at football matches has changed beyond recognition. Partly this is because it is harder to sing when sitting down, but also because rising ticket prices have forced out younger and more vocal supporters. Manchester United's captain Roy Keane famously derided the new breed of passive, corporate spectators as the 'prawn sandwich brigade'. Others dubbed the stadium 'Cold Trafford'.

Extensive reconstruction as a result of the Taylor Report has also led to the loss of hundreds of old stands and venues, with all

the concomitant sense of loss that such breaks with the past often elicit (even though the majority of condemned structures have been of little or no architectural merit).

Among the losses in the Manchester area have been Oldham RLFC's Watersheddings Ground, in 1996, and Bolton Wanderer's Burnden Park, in 1997.

Also, because one seat takes up an area equivalent to two standing positions, and because seating tiers require steeper rakes than terraces to ensure adequate sightlines, the sheer physical mass of new stands is considerably greater. Compare, for example, the views of Old Trafford on pp 28-29. The earlier ground squeezed in 77,000, when the majority were standing, whereas the current stadium, once redevelopment is complete, will reach 75,000, but on a footprint twice the size, and with stands more than three times the height of the originals.

Yet there have been positive consequences too. The Taylor Report forced clubs to re-evaluate completely their facilities and crowd management operations. There can be no doubt that venues

are far safer and better managed than ever before. (Lord Justice Taylor commented wryly that his report was intended not to prepare football for the 21st century so much as to drag it into the 20th.)

In addition, Old Trafford, the City of Manchester Stadium, and other new venues such as Bolton's stunning Reebok Stadium (opened 1997), are all better geared towards the needs of women, children and spectators with disabilities.

From the examples illustrated in this chapter, one key conservation issue arises.

Unlike former swimming pools, for example, once a stadium or ground is deemed surplus to requirements there are few options for adaptive re-use. Sites are usually therefore sold to help fund their replacements.

However, as traditional terraces formed such an important part of so many people's lives in the last century, is there a case for conserving at least one, as a relic if not as a functioning terrace?

Given the pace of change in the post-Taylor world, it is a question that we should at least address, sooner rather than later.

In Manchester only one senior ground retains terraces; the Willows (*above left*), home of Salford Reds RLFC. The Reds are currently planning a new stadium, (*see p61*), but may retain the Willows for community use. If this were to occur, the Shed (*on the far touchline*), dating from 1935, might be ideal for preservation as an example of a typical 20th century terrace. There are, meanwhile, no memorials at all for Station Road (*above*), the former home of Swinton RLFC, sold for redevelopment in 1992. Since then Swinton have shared at Gigg Lane, Moor Lane and currently at Sedgley Park, Whitefield. To be homeless is one of the worst fates that can befall a sports club.

▲ A typical inner-city ground of the 20th century. This was Manchester City's **Maine Road**, Moss Side, two years before its demolition in 2003. When opened in 1923 the surrounding houses were all in place, yet for sure, none of the residents was consulted.

Maine Road is Manchester's most thoroughly documented sports venue, thanks to club historian, Gary James, whose *Farewell to Maine Road* (see *Links*) is strongly recommended. Briefly however, after finally rejecting a move to Belle Vue (see *chapter 4*) City's directors shocked everyone, not only by moving from east Manchester to this former tip and clay pit, but also by building a stadium twice the size of the club's previous, cramped 40,000 capacity ground at Hyde Road.

Maine Road's architect was Charles Swain, whose work included various theatres and cinemas, including the Queen's Theatre, Great Bridgewater Street, and the Kinemacolor Palace on Whitworth Street (now part of the Cornerhouse complex). The contractors were Sir Robert McAlpine & Co., who were building Wembley at the same time.

Although in its final years as an all-seated venue the capacity was just under 35,000, Maine Road holds a record that is unlikely to be beaten, for the largest gate at an English club ground. This was in March 1934 when 84,569 attended an FA Cup tie v. Stoke.

Although Swain's original masterplan had been well thought out, from the 1960s onwards Maine Road became a classic example of ill-considered, piecemeal development: each new stand differing from its neighbour in form and scale; none of the corners or roof lines quite matching.

Despite this jarring clash of styles, Maine Road was held in deep affection by its long suffering regulars, particularly those on its popular terrace, the Kippax (named after a nearby street).

City's departure in 2003 was not the end of their involvement in Moss Side. Their Platt Lane training complex, run jointly with Manchester City Council, is one of the finest club-based community sports facilties in Britain.

A further reminder of City's presence is a nearby estate whose streets are named after former Blues, such as Frank Swift, Sammy Cookson and (*left*) Billy Meredith.

▶ Formed in 1861 and therefore one of Britain's oldest rugby clubs, **Sale RFC** first played at their **Heywood Road** ground in 1905. The club have helped put Sale on the map and are part and parcel of the local scene.

Since joining the ranks of rugby union's newly professionalised clubs in 1996, however – as the **Sale Sharks** – the club directors have concluded that Heywood Road's suburban setting can no longer accommodate their needs. In 2003 therefore the Sharks switched their Zurich Premiership matches to Stockport's Edgeley Park, which has 9,500 seats, double the total at Heywood Road.

Crowds have risen accordingly, and Heywood Road has at least been retained as the club's base and for use by Sale's amateur and junior teams. But the first XV has moved on, thus breaking a 142 year old link with the host community. Such is progress.

One of several fellow rugby clubs facing similar issues is **Salford Reds RLFC**; their own ground, **The Willows**, set albeit rather differently from Sale, in the working class district of Weaste (*centre right*).

If rugby union's abrupt embrace of professionalism was a shock to the system, so too was rugby league's decision, also in 1996, to broaden its appeal by switching the season from winter to summer.

Some critics have condemned this and other moves towards modernisation as a misguided attempt to escape the game's cloth cap roots. Others counter that it is 'do or die' for what is essentially a minority, regionally based sport.

Opened in 1901, the Willows is undoubtedly a problematic site, restricted on two sides and with a capacity of 10,800. That is lower than many of the Reds' rivals, such as Hull and Wigan, who have purpose-built modern stadiums. The accommodation is also of a poorer quality, and therefore yields less income.

Keen to remain one of rugby league's elite clubs, the Reds have therefore combined with other commercial interests to propose a 240 acre stadium, hotel, office and retail park on their former training ground at Barton, opposite the aerodrome (*see p115*).

If all goes to plan, the 20,000 capacity stadium (*below right*) designed by Arup Sport (architects of the City of Manchester Stadium), will open in 2006. Intriguingly, this could be the first major post-Taylor stadium to incorporate modern terraces, as requested by the fans.

Also, as the new stadium will be financed entirely by its associated commercial developments, the Reds hope, like Sale, not to sell their old ground but to retain it for local and community use.

▲ Pictured here in the mid 1950s, the **Fallowfield Stadium** was Manchester's first permanent home for athletics and cycling. It was also one of the unlikeliest of locations for a stadium, accessed via a path off Whitworth Lane, in what was then an almost rural hinterland between Rusholme and Ladybarn.

Opened in May 1892, it was laid out by the **Manchester Athletic Club**, whose previous base at Old Trafford (see p26) had been purchased for redevelopment. The stadium also became the venue for the annual race meets of the **Manchester Wheelers**, one of many clubs to form during the cycling boom of the late 19th century. (At one gathering in Alexandra Park in 1883 some 50,000 spectators were reported as in attendance.)

However it was football which first put Fallowfield on the map, when the stadium infamously hosted the March 1893 FA Cup Final between Everton and Wolverhampton Wanderers (after the usual venue, the Oval in London, had become suddenly unavailable). Although the terraces, pavilion and single stand could accommodate 15,000 at most, over 45,000 fans converged on this quiet backwater. Precious few were able to see and it was only by luck that no serious injuries resulted from the prevailing disorder.

Despite this debacle, amazingly the FA awarded Fallowfield a second game; a semi-final in 1899 between Sheffield United and Liverpool. This time the game was abandoned owing to the crush.

Less chaotically Fallowfield was also tried for rugby, including an England v. Scotland match in 1897 – a fixture that has been played in London ever since – and two Northern Union Challenge Cup Finals, in 1899 and 1900. It also hosted various rugby clubs, among them Broughton Park.

Two Amateur Athletics Association championships were staged at Fallowfield, in 1897 and 1907, and in 1910 a crowd of 20,000 gathered to see the aviator Claude Grahame-White take off from the infield during the annual Manchester Wheelers Race Meet.

These race meets were Fallowfield's longest established fixture, drawing large crowds until interest tailed off in the 1950s.

Before then the stadium had staged the 1919 national cycling championships, and in 1934 the cycle races for that year's British Empire Games (since renamed the Commonwealth Games), even though London's White City was the Games' main venue.

In 1955 Reg Harris, the greatest Wheeler ever (see p55), helped purchase Fallowfield from the Manchester AC, and for a period it was renamed the Reg Harris Stadium. But it could never pay its way – no private athletics or cycling venue has ever done so – and in the early 1960s the site was sold to the ever expanding university, whose Firs Athletic Ground (see p74) bordered the stadium

As the track deteriorated, Fallowfield staged its final Wheelers meet in 1976, and in 1994, despite opposition from residents and cycling enthusiasts, the stadium was cleared to make way for halls of residence.

No public memorial to the stadium's 102 year long history marks the site.

▷ One of the harsh realities of athletics is that while public and media interest for international events such as the Olympics and World Championships remains intense – the City of Manchester Stadium was 99.7 per cent sold out for the Commonwealth Games in 2002 – on a national and local level attendances are modest.

Britain's largest athletics venue, Don Valley Stadium, Sheffield, holds 25,000 but is rarely filled, while if London wins the right to stage the 2012 Olympics, after the Games it is proposed to downsize the main stadium from 80,000 seats to less than 30,000.

But if popularity were to be measured in terms of the number of meetings held and athletes participating, then Britain's leading facility is quite probably the little known **Longford Park Stadium**, Ryebank Road, Chorlton.

Tucked away behind trees in a corner of Longford Park – formerly the grounds of Longford Hall, built by the cotton merchant John Rylands in 1857 and purchased by Stretford Urban District Council in 1911 – this popular stadium, which opened in 1964 and has a single stand for 700 spectators, stages over 50 meetings a year. Training sessions on the track also attract up to 150-200 athletes every evening during the season.

What makes the stadium doubly remarkable is that while it is owned by Trafford Metropolitan Borough Council, it is actually managed by the stadium's resident club, **Trafford Athletics Club**. No other athletics club in the country bears such a responsibility. Better still, during the 1990s the club raised sufficient funds to build their own fitness centre and conference suite, which helps to finance their running costs.

Their effort has clearly been rewarded. Having been represented at every Olympic Games since 1968, Trafford is now the north of England's most successful club, its chief rivals being Sale Harriers, based at Wythenshawe Park.

With two such strong clubs in the city – and let us not forget the legendary Salford Harriers, based at Boggart Hole Clough – it might seem odd that since the demise of Fallowfield, Manchester's largest athletics venue is the Manchester Regional Arena at Sportcity (*see p54*), with just 6,000 seats.

Yet, to be blunt, that is probably sufficient. For as Longford Park demonstrates, for most athletes, most of the time, it is work done away from the limelight that achieves the best results in the end.

More than 70 athletes who have represented Britain at international level have started their careers on this track, which is one of several sports facilities within Longford Park. A typical synthetic track for local authority usage will last 7-10 years, and cost £110-120,000 to replace, about half the cost of the type used in an Olympic stadium.

Chapter Seven

Turnstiles

The nameplate of an Ellison's turnstile at the Victoria Baths, Hathersage Road. There was a time when virtually every swimming baths in the country had Salford-made turnstiles. Those at Hathersage Road are the originals, installed when the building opened in 1906.

From the mid 1890s until at least the 1980s, the vast majority of turnstiles fitted at British stadiums, sports grounds, racecourses, swimming pools, piers, zoos, parks, gardens, fairgrounds, exhibition halls, ferry terminals, even public toilets, were manufactured in Manchester.

Or, to be more precise, in Salford, by two engineering companies, WT Ellison and Co., and WH Bailey Ltd.

This is no small matter. During the 19th century it needed the invention of numerous, ostensibly mundane products and devices to enable sport to blossom into the spectacle we know today.

The lawnmower, for example, invented in Gloucestershire in 1830, facilitated the creation of smooth turf and therefore swifter ball games. The Acme Thunderer, first made in Birmingham in 1884, allowed referees to whistle above the roar of the crowd without straining their lungs.

But the humble turnstile played one of the most crucial roles of all in the forward march of mass spectator sport during the late 19th

century, and that was to provide a simple but reasonably secure means by which clubs could take cash on the door.

The more efficiently a club could do this, the more it could afford to sign skilled players, improve its facilities and, thereby, compete at the highest possible level afforded by its 'gate'.

The earliest known reference to turnstiles at a sports venue is in the *Wisden Cricketer's Almanack* of 1871, where the new turnstiles at Lord's were dubbed 'tell-tales', because, theoretically, they prevented people entering without payment.

But the earliest actual turnstile surviving today dates from ten years later, in 1881. It was made in London by the Southwark firm of Stevens and Sons, for Southend Pier, although it was salvaged from Southend United's ground in the 1970s. Three 1885 Stevens turnstiles were found at Shrewsbury Town in the 1980s, and there is an 1887 'Silent Reversible' Stevens, thought to come from the Oval cricket ground, on display at the *Homes of Football* Gallery in Ambleside.

Another London manufacturer was Norton & Co., who sold units to cricket grounds as far afield as Sydney and Hobart in the 1880s.

Most of these companies' clients would have been seaside piers, zoos and amusement parks, such as Belle Vue and Crystal Palace. But as attendances at sporting events surged from the 1890s onwards – particularly at football, rugby, cricket and racing – the turnstile market suddenly took off.

Football clubs in particular had become increasingly concerned that their own, basic payboxes were too susceptible to fraud. One such club, Aston Villa, even hired private detectives to nail their suspect gatemen.

Fortunately, a Salford-based engineer was on the case.

The DeLuce Patented 'Rush Preventive' Turnstile, manufactured by WT Ellison and Co. of Irlams o'th' Height, was exactly the right product at the right time.

William Ellison, of Camp Street, Lower Broughton, established his business to make steam pumps »

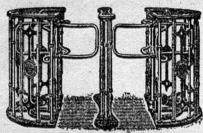

RUSH PREVENTIVE
ELLISON'S PATENT TURNSTILES
With All Latest Improvements

The only **RELIABLE MACHINE**

BUY NO OTHERS.

No matter how cheap a Turnstile may be it is NO USE unless ACCURATE.
Are unequalled for **DURABILITY, ACCURACY, and FINISH.**

The following List of Clubs and Racecourses, among others, that have
been supplied by us will show that we are the Leading Makers of
Turnstiles, and have a world-wide reputation.

Racecourses.		Sheffield Wedns'y	Clyde
Manchester	Wembley Stadium	Manchester United	Aberdeen
Haydock Park	White City, M/c.	Barnsley	Scottish
Birmingham	**Association**	Hull City	Football Union
Chester	**Football Clubs.**	West Bromwich A.	Hamilton
Keele Park	Everton	Southampton	Academicals
Aintree	Liverpool	Preston North End	Heart of
Newmarket	Stoke City	Wolverhampton W.	Midlothian, &c
Stockton	Glossop	Leeds United	**Irish**
Redcar	Bury	Birmingham	**Football Clubs.**
Leicester	Aston Villa	Brierley Hill A.	Glentoran
Hooton Park, &c.	Bristol Rovers	Middlesbrough	Distillery
Greyhound Courses.	Bristol City	Crewe Alexandra	Cliftonville
Bristol	Brentford	Newcastle United,	Shelbourne
Belfast	Chelsea	&c.	Belfast Celtic
Birmingham	Fulham	**Scottish**	Bohemian, &c.
Bolton	Tottenham H.	**Football Clubs.**	**Rugby**
Blackpool	Southport	Celtic	**Football Clubs.**
Cardiff	Sunderland	Kilmarnock	Salford
Glasgow	Bolton Wanderers	Queen's Park	Leicester
Harringay	Sheffield United	St. Mirren	Broughton R.
Liverpool	The Arsenal	Glasgow Rangers	Oldham
Manchester	Portsmouth	Falkirk	Warrington
Sheffield	Blackburn Rovers	Morton	Leeds
Salford	Derby County	Ayr United	Hull K'gston R.
White City,	Notts County	Dundee	Swinton
London	Notts Forest	Airdrieonians	Wigan, &c.
	Manchester City		

We supplied **THE BRITISH EMPIRE EXHIBITION** (1924)
STADIUM AND WEMBLEY AMUSEMENTS with the WHOLE of
their Turnstiles. A Total of 354 TURNSTILES and 25 EXIT CAGES.
Also EMPIRE EXHIBITION, GLASGOW, 1938.

Prices on application.   *Send for Testimonials.*

W. T. ELLISON & CO., Ltd., ENGINEERS,
PENDLETON, SALFORD 6, LANCS.
Telegrams and Cables : " TURNSTILES, MANCHESTER."
Telephone : No. 2030 PENDLETON.

▲ Samuel Alfred Nelson DeLuce, believed to have haled from Huguenot stock, was about 29 years old when he started at Ellison's in approximately 1895. DeLuce claimed that each 'Rush Preventive' turnstile could process 4,000 entrants per hour, or 3,000 if change had to be sorted.

Nowadays the maximum rate used for calculating the number of turnstiles needed in any particular part of a venue is a mere 660 per hour, and all counting is done by computer.

After launching the turnstile in 1895, Ellison's went on to manufacture ticket machines for cinemas and the ubiquitous 'penny-in-the-slot' door mechanisms for public toilets (from which we derive the saying 'to spend a penny').

Apparently DeLuce would often describe his embarrassment when caught once in a ladies toilet in Southport, checking one of his company's installations.

Ellison's advertisement (*left*) from the *Athletic News Football Annual* for 1937-38 lists every professional sports venue in Manchester as a client of the company.

▲ An **Ellison's coverplate**, c.1914, at Hearts FC, Edinburgh. Earlier models bore the address Irlams o'th'Height rather than Salford, and were stamped 'preventive' rather than 'preventative'.

Under the glass cover was a finely engineered brass unit (*above right*) with ceramic counters. Shown here is one from Villa Park, Birmingham, dating from c.1895.

Once screwed into position under the coverplate, lead seals were placed over the screw heads – inside the two lugs seen above – in order to prevent tampering. These

seals were one of the first things a tax inspector would look for in cases where clubs were suspected of underpaying entertainment tax, introduced in 1917.

When it came to defrauding the clubs themselves, operators were known to disconnect the counters from the frame, or smash the counter glass in order to insert a screwdriver and stop the counter.

The counters' solid brass fittings also made turnstiles a prime target for thieves. On one infamous night in Glasgow apparently 40 coverplates were stolen.

WT Ellison occupied the same modest works at 323, Bolton Road, throughout its lifetime, from 1893 to 1963. Here the staff are assembling double-pattern turnstiles for the Battersea Funfair in 1951.

》 originally, in around 1893. But it appears to have been his works manager, Sam DeLuce, who, two years later, designed the turnstile that would shape Ellison's future.

Selling for £7 2s 6d each, the 'Rush Preventive' was a standard revolving turnstile, but with two added checks. Firstly, a foot pedal allowed the operator to lock and unlock the turning spindle arm as each entrant paid and passed through. Thus, theoretically, only one person could enter at a time. Rushes were prevented.

Secondly, unlike their rivals, Ellison's provided tamper-proof counters, so that officials could tally the numbers admitted against the sums collected.

Needless to say, the design was not foolproof. With the connivance of the operator youngsters could slide over or under the bars. Also, by carefully timing the release of the pedal the operator could engineer a narrow gap through which two or more people might squeeze – or whole groups of workmates and families if folklore is to be believed!

But overall, Ellison's clients found that their gate receipts rose considerably – embarrassingly so in some cases – once the turnstiles were in place.

From 1895 onwards, Ellison's list of clients read like an inventory of the British leisure industry.

It included every major sports ground and swimming bath in Manchester and Salford, plus Wembley Stadium (which had exactly 100 Ellison turnstiles when opened in 1923), Hampden Park, Aintree Racecourse, Wimbledon, Twickenham, Murrayfield and two of Blackpool's three piers.

The turnstiles at the 1951 Festival of Britain exhibition and at Battersea Funfair were also Ellison's.

Inspired by the news of this last order, in 1950 readers of the *Salford City Reporter* wrote in with their own unusual sitings of Ellison turnstiles around the globe.

In Britain this included a ferry in Plymouth, Sandringham Castle and Swallow Falls in north Wales. Among the overseas locations noted were Cairo Zoo, 》

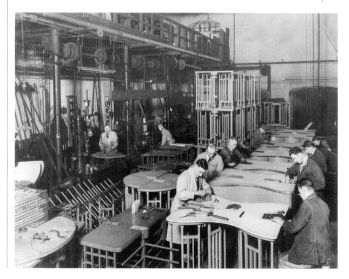

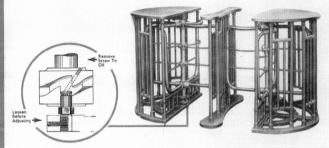

ELLISON'S

HEAVY DEEP CONVEX ARM TURNSTILES

Ellison's "Rush-preventive" Footstep Motion

This footstep is fitted to all our turnstiles and ensures free rotation of the spindle on ball bearings which may be lubricated by removing the oiling screw.

The spindle may be raised or lowered to compensate for wear by adjusting the hexagon nut as shown.

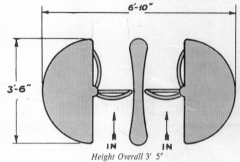

Height Overall 3' 5"

The illustration shows two registering Turnstiles and one Barrier. This type of Turnstile has been specially designed with extra deep convex arms to prevent creeping underneath and also more than one person passing through for each payment. They are most effective in separating the crowd into units and are highly recommended where great rushes are anticipated.

Can be supplied registering only, controlled by footlever, or non-registering for exit only.

Approximate Weights:—
Turnstiles 4 cwt. each.
Barriers 2 cwt. each.

Prices on application.

Series No. 6

W. T. ELLISON & COMPANY LIMITED
Turnstile Specialists
3·2·3 BOLTON ROAD · PENDLETON · SALFORD 6 · LANCS
Telephone: Pen 2030   Telegrams: Turnstiles, Manchester

◄ A company advertisement from the late 1950s shows how little the design changed over the years. But why change a winning formula? At least four of the thirteen Ellison's still in use at Manchester City's Maine Road, before the ground was demolished in 2003, were thought to have dated from 1896, while Withington Baths still has its original installation from 1913 (*see p4*). Countless more examples from the inter-war period remain can be found in use all over Britain. Manchester United's museum has a rare 1950s model which, as the advert states, operated both ways, for entry and exit.

▲ The turnstile manufacturing division of **WH Bailey** (a much larger engineering enterprise) was based at the Albion Works, Patricroft. The firm was established long before Ellison's, in 1839, but despite the advertisement's claim, did not start making turnstiles until 1930. By the end of the 1940s, it has been estimated, there were at least 9,000 Ellison and Bailey turnstiles in use in Britain alone. Some clubs, including Manchester City, mixed and matched both makes within their grounds.

» several stadiums in both Italy and the United States and, rather ominously, South Africa, where they were supplied in cages to a number of gold and diamond mines in order for 'native workers' to be checked after each shift.

On a brighter note there were also Ellison's at the Hong Kong ferry terminal, where they made a fleeting appearance in the 1955 Clark Gable film *Soldier of Fortune*.

Ellison's was by all acounts a friendly, family firm.

It never moved from its original premises, a former stable at 323 Bolton Road, with a foundry at the rear, and rarely employed more than 50-60 workers, even at its peak.

Two factors led to its downfall.

The turnstile market itself declined during the post-war period, partly because very little sports ground development took place, and partly because the pre-1939 turnstiles were so durable.

But the final nail in Ellison's coffin was the 1963 Public Lavatories (Turnstiles) Act, described at the time as Barbara Castle's Act (although it was a Unionist MP, Patricia McLaughlin who led the campaign).

The end of charging for toilets meant the end of one of Ellison's other best sellers, the penny-in-the-slot door mechanisms.

Ellison's finally closed its doors in March 1963.

The Manchester area's links with the industry were not severed, however. Bailey's continued for a few years, while a former Ellison's manager continued production at Farnworth, then Ashton-under-Lyne, under the name of Mayor Ltd. This company merged with a Swedish firm, Gunnebo, in 1996, which continues to make turnstiles today (although production ended at Ashton in 2000).

But still the link continues, for one of Britain's current leading manufacturers of turnstiles for stadiums – including at Old Trafford and the City of Manchester Stadium – is Broughton Controls, based just up the road in Oldham.

▲ Turnstile blocks, as these two excellent examples from Manchester venues demonstrate, provide architects with tremendous scope to set the tone for the spectacle on offer.

The fastidious and handsome 1930s block at **Old Trafford** cricket ground, on Warwick Road (*above left*) houses six Ellison turnstiles and is still in use today, while **Belle Vue** greyhound stadium's more exuberant design (*above*), on the corner of Kirkmanshulme Lane and Mount Road, from the early 1960s, doubles as an advert for the racy pleasures within.

Alas the block is now disused and lies hidden behind advertisement hoardings.

Some industry insiders dislike the use of turnstiles in modern venues. They argue that turnstile blocks can be gloomy and intimidating. So, at the City of Manchester Stadium, for example, season ticket holders now use plastic cards to open low-level barriers (as is now common on the London Underground).

With all-ticketed, all-seated matches increasingly becoming the norm, and CCTV cameras monitoring all spectators' behaviour on entry, the need for old fashioned turnstiles will almost certainly recede in the coming years. In time it may simply be a matter of having each person's retina or fingerprint read as they cross the threshold.

But for those who still have cause to pass through a dimly-lit, 20th century turnstile block – cool ironwork pressing against one's thigh, anonymous fingers reaching out through a small gap in the mesh, a metallic 'clunk' announcing one's arrival – the turnstile remains a powerful cultural experience; a rite of passage even, marking the transition from the real world into the fantasy realm of sport.

Whilst dwelling on this thought the next time you pass through such a turnstile, look down at the coverplate and at the design of the metalwork generally.

Chances are that if it looks old, it will almost certainly have been made in Salford.

Chapter Eight

Clubs and Pavilions

Earning their stripes – the Manchester Football Club 1st XV pose in front of their pavilion in Whalley Range, in 1872. The ground lay between Kings Road, Ayres Road, St John's Road and Darnley Street. Formed in 1860 by ex-public school boys, Manchester FC were not only the city's first football club – albeit it was rugby football they played, the so-called 'hacking game' – but also the first rugby club in the north of England. Subsequently based at Moor Lane (see p37), the club is now at Grove Park, Cheadle Hulme. Because most early clubs rented their grounds, pavilions tended to be cheap, timber-framed and of a temporary nature. Modernity was seldom afforded, and seldom desired.

Sports clubs are the very heart and soul of sporting activity in Britain; not just the high profile ones we know so much about from the media but the estimated 110,000 voluntary clubs, or CASCs in modern parlance (Community Amateur Sports Clubs), which, according to the Central Council of Physical Recreation, have a combined membership in excess of 5.6 million.

The typical CASC is run entirely by volunteers. At one Manchester club, for example, a teacher tends the wicket. A bricklayer nurses the bowling greens. The bar is managed by a retired clerical officer while his wife deals with catering and cleaning. The club runs no fewer than 14 teams, for both sexes and for age groups ranging from 8-50.

As emphasised earlier, these volunteers also play a key role as unofficial guardians of a significant proportion of our urban open space. The club mentioned above owns 11 acres.

The Manchester area has a dense concentration of such clubs. In outdoor sports alone there are over 800 for football – the highest number per capita anywhere in England – over 300 for bowls, plus dozens more for rugby, cricket, tennis, golf, lacrosse, athletics, hockey and archery.

Not all own, or even have exclusive use of their own grounds or premises. Of those that do, very few have buildings of any architectural merit (a judgement which applies across Britain, not only to Manchester).

Yet never before have there been so many financial breaks for sports clubs wanting to improve their facilities; for example via Sport England's Community Investment Fund (worth £11.3 million in the north west for the period 2002-09), or courtesy of a new Inland Revenue scheme for CASCs which confers a package of tax benefits plus substantial reductions in business rates.

Underpinning this array of schemes are a welter of design guidelines for *new* facilities, drawn up by Sport England, by the Commission for Architecture and the Built Environment, and by individual governing bodies.

But for the occupants of older or historic premises, no specific guidance exists. Nor, when it comes to meeting ever demanding building regulations or when adapting creaking dressing rooms, or patching up leaking roofs, may such clubs draw on separate Lottery funds.

It should therefore be no surprise that pragmatism – the installation of unsympathetic replacement windows, for example, or the addition of incongruous extensions – takes precedence over conservation in most clubs' list of priorities.

Nor, in truth, is 'old' always synonymous with 'good'.

Yet Manchester possesses several genuinely historic clubhouses and pavilions, and the local sports scene would patently be much the poorer were all to be lost or insensitively redeveloped in the scramble for survival and modernisation.

Indeed if sports clubs are the very heart and soul of sporting activity in Britain, it is surely at grass roots level that our sporting heritage is at its most precious.

As Manchester's suburbs expanded from the mid 19th century onwards, a number of private sports clubs were laid out, often in the open spaces left between the back gardens of houses built around a grid of four streets. Bowls and lawn tennis (which overtook croquet in popularity from the 1880s) were most common, both being playable on relatively compact lawns.

The **Albert Bowls and Tennis Club** on Old Lansdowne Road, West Didsbury (*left*) is a typical example. Opened in 1874 as a gentlemen's bowls club and now part of the Albert Park Conservation Area, it retains its original red brick clubhouse with typical black and white timber detailing and offers facilities for table tennis, snooker and darts, plus a bar and social area on which the club largely depends for survival. On the clubhouse's south side is a crown green bowling lawn. On its north side are six all-weather tennis courts. Over 400 members pay annual fees ranging between £8 for pensioners up to £90 for adults.

Also noteworthy is the bowls and tennis club forming the central hub of the **Burnage Garden Estate** (*below left*), bordered by North Avenue, West Avenue, East Avenue and South Avenue, Burnage.

Built between 1906 and 1911 as a private co-operative housing scheme, and comprising 138 houses in a stripped Arts and Crafts style, this remarkable – and, judging from residents' comments, seemingly contented – enclave was designed by J Horner Hargreaves in consultation with CG Agate, FB Dunkerley and the doyen of the garden suburb movement, Raymond Unwin.

Unlike its Manchester contemporary, Chorltonville, which has since been broken up into private ownership, the Burnage estate is still managed and owned by a single entity, the Manchester Tenants Co-operative.

All residents have free use of the sports facilities, a community hall and children's playground, and the inner ring of houses all have gardens backing onto the sports facilities.

Unsurprisingly there is a long waiting list for would-be tenants.

▲ In almost every corner of Britain examples of the homely, vernacular style preferred by Victorian sports clubs can be found. Above is the **Ladies Pavilion**, built in 1883 in the grounds of **Davyhulme Hall** (in modern day Trafford). Robert Henry Norreys, the Hall's owner, had created for his friends a private sporting paradise, with a small racecourse, an archery ground and a nine hole golf course, for whose female regulars the pavilion was intended (even though there were only 30 of them at the time).

Davyhulme Hall was demolished in 1888, but the course survived and in 1911 the current **Davyhulme Park Golf Club** formed there. Its distinctive 1930s clubhouse is shown on page 75.

The Ladies Pavilion, meanwhile, became a tenanted cottage in 1902 and is now a private home.

Three miles due north is the **Ellesmere Sports Ground**, Walkden Road, formerly part of the extensive estates belonging to the 3rd Duke of Bridgewater, of Worsley Old Hall. It was the Duke who, in 1751, famously completed Britain's first man made canal. He left no heirs, however, and so in 1803

his estate was bequeathed under trust to Lord Francis Egerton, who in 1846 was made the first Earl of Ellesmere, and whose family – great benefactors in the Worsley area generally – laid out the sports ground c.1868.

Worsley Cricket Club, formed by local stonemasons in 1846 and sponsored by the Earl, have played there ever since. The club pavilion (*above right*) dates from c.1900, but has been extended and altered since, particularly by the addition of pebbledash in the 1950s. It nevertheless retains a great charm, as does the ground. After a visit in 1900 Archie MacLaren, the Lancashire and England cricketer, called it the prettiest in England.

On the other side of cricket pitch stands the clubhouse of the **Ellesmere Sports Club**, built in 1932 (after its original pavilion burnt down), looking out over greens for bowls and croquet. There are also facilities for squash and tennis. Ellesmere SC and Worsley CC merged their facilities in 1973.

But perhaps most picturesque of all on this historic sports ground is the small but perfectly formed timber pavilion known to all as

Lord Ellesmere's Hut (*above*). This was erected in 1890 for the 3rd Earl of Ellesmere to watch his son and heir, John Francis Granville Scrope Egerton, aka Lord Brackley, play cricket (at which he was good enough to captain the MCC). After a few years doubling as the cricket score box the hut was re-erected in another part of the ground, where it now serves as the croquet pavilion.

▶ On Stableford Avenue, Monton Green, also within the former estate of the sports-loving Ellesmere family, is the **Worsley Golf Club** (no part of which, oddly enough, actually lies in Worsley).

Formed in 1894 with the 3rd Earl of Ellesmere (*whose personal hut is pictured below left*) as its first president, the golf club's distinctive timber-framed clubhouse (*right*) is typical in that, for all its traditional appeal, its fabric has proved to be a constant drain upon the members' time and resources.

In terms that will be familiar to many a weary club official, Worsley's history (*see Links*) affectionately recounts the frustrations its Building Committee has encountered as it has struggled over the years to maintain and improve the pavilion – whose core dates back to 1897 – amid regular tussles with the Finance Committee and with the club's more conservative members, even down to 'petty arguments' about where to position the honours boards.

Amongst the routine problems faced by Worsley have been flooding from a nearby brook, dry rot on the verandah, short circuiting electrics, fetid drains, leaking roofs, infestations of insects and rodents, and, in recent years, vandalism.

Two further challenges have been to keep in step with building regulations and to maximise the pavilion's earning capacity. The rather awkward, but vital single storey dining room extension seen on the right of the clubhouse, added in 1959, was budgeted at £3,000 but ended up costing over £11,000. In the 1980s it was found necessary to find £72,000 for basic remedial work.

In short, historic clubhouses are for many self-financed clubs a curse as well as a blessing.

Still clinging to the half-timbered look was the substantial pavilion of the **Co-operative Wholesale Society** sports ground on Victoria Avenue, Moston (*shown above in 1969*), known as Tudor Lodge and opened within a few years of the ground's purchase in 1928. CWS offered employees facilities for football, cricket, hockey, tennis, bowls and athletics, in return for a small annual subscription of 2-3s, according to the sport, plus 1d a week for the ground's upkeep.

Like most works grounds, declining interest amongst the staff led to the site's sale, in 1998, although the pitches and pavilion are still in use by the **North Manchester and Oldham Colleges Rugby Club**, and by the **Assheton Bowmen** (*see p77*).

▲ The pavilion of the **Firs Athletic Ground**, Moseley Road, Fallowfield, was originally built for Owens College (now Manchester University) at the turn of the 20th century. Owens College had been established in 1851 by a bequest from the non-conformist cotton merchant, John Owens (1790-1846), who insisted that no religious, financial or class barriers be raised to intending students, as long as they were male and aged over fourteen. Women were admitted after 1883.

A male-only Athletics Union formed at the college two years later but had no grounds of its own until 1898, when the trustees of Sir Joseph Whitworth donated ten acres of the Firs Estate. Members of the university then purchased an extra 42 acres, of which 14 were sold on for development in order to finance the ground's layout and the construction of the pavilion.

A £3,000 donation from Tootal Broadhurst, the cotton goods manufacturers, helped complete the project.

The core of the pavilion – red brick with timber facings, an octagonal clock tower and a viewing terrace – almost certainly dates from this period, c. 1900.

The building was then extended in 1922 by two university staff members, Professor AC Dickie and J McGregor, to provide additional facilities for women.

This in itself is noteworthy, for although a Woman's Athletic Union had formed at the college in 1900, it was not until after the First World War that female athletes competed at their own events. The world's first women's international meeting was staged in 1921, in Monte Carlo. The following year the Women's Amateur Athletic Association was formed.

The pavilion's 1922 extension thus marks a modest, but significant turning point in the history of Manchester athletics.

The Firs today includes a late 20th century sports hall, an athletics track and various pitches laid out for football, lacrosse, cricket and other sports.

▲ The pristine clubhouse of **Davyhulme Park Golf Club,** Gleneagles Road, Davyhulme, is a rare example of a 1930s sports building in the Manchester area.

Designed in modernist style by AE McCutcheon and club member AN Potter (a borough surveyor who also worked on the nearby Urmston Baths, *see p126*), the clubhouse cost £10,365 and was opened by local MP Anthony Crossley in March 1937.

It featured maple floors, a terrazzo staircase, a large dining area, a telephone kiosk, two billiard tables, a card room, a committee room, plus all the usual changing rooms, offices, bars and a kitchen, fitted with an Aga cooker.

As is common with buildings of this period the original Tailby metal framed windows have been replaced by PVC windows. A retro-style clockface was also added to the south facing elevation in 2000.

Otherwise the building is relatively intact and is one of only a handful of 1930s clubhouses extant in Britain, among them the Royal Birkdale Golf Club, Southport (1935) and Childwall Golf Club, near Liverpool (1938).

Although golf as a sport is sometimes criticised for its impact on historic landscapes and upon the environment, a number of golf clubs around Britain have actually helped preserve important buildings by converting them into

clubhouses. A measure of this is that of 63 golf-related properties on the register of listed buildings, it is thought only two were built specifically for golf.

Examples of this adaptive re-use include the **Manchester Golf Club** (formerly based at Trafford Hall, *see p26*), whose clubhouse is built around the 18th century Hopwood Cottage, on Rochdale Road, Middleton, and the **Chorlton-Cum-Hardy Golf Club**, Barlow Hall Road, whose club house is Barlow Hall, a Grade II listed building with elements dating from the 16th century. The course itself was formerly part of Barlow Moor, used as a race course in the 17th century (*see p36*).

Chapter Nine

Archery

Target archery at the Eccles Archery Club, Peel Green Road. Each target is printed on a disposable sheet of paper and attached to a four foot diameter 'boss' made of densely woven straw. The colours – known as the Prince's Colours – have not altered since the early 19th century, when the Prince Regent helped revive the sport's popularity.

Archery is one of Britain's longest established, organised sports. The earliest recorded club dates back to Scotland in the 15th century, while the oldest, continuously staged tournament, the Scorton Arrow, originated in Yorkshire in 1673.

Archery clubs nowadays mostly share premises and grounds with other sports clubs. But even though the sport lacks an architectural legacy of its own, such are archery's longstanding associations with the area – at least three societies formed in the late 18th century, and over 30 are currently active in the north west – that, as is the case with lacrosse, no study of sporting heritage in Manchester could possibly overlook its history.

The sport's origins lie of course in hunting and warfare. From approximately 1300-1580 the longbow formed the mainstay of the English army, famed for its blistering use against the French at Cressy and Agincourt. Closer to home, the Middleton Archers scored a decisive victory at Flodden Field in 1513 (*see right*).

Maintaining the skills of England's famed and feared longbowmen was a perennial challenge for the authorities.

As can be imagined, some individuals hardly needed encouragement. Expertise with the bow was a sure sign of manliness. But from at least 1349 onwards a succession of court orders was deemed necessary to force men to practise at the butts every week. (The term butts refers both to the practice ground itself and to the actual targets, set up on mounds of earth or stone. Street names such as Butts Lane or The Butts often indicate their location.)

Some court orders threatened fines for failure to practise. Others sought to ban sports such as bowls and rabbit coursing that were seen as likely distractions. (Wealthy individuals were naturally exempt from such orders.)

From 16th century Court Leet records we know that Manchester's butts were situated in Alport Lane, in the Castlefield area. In 1576 these butts had to be repaired after being damaged by stray cattle. Two years later the

local court ordered constables to list those men who either had no bow or arrows, or who possessed equipment but chose not to practise. 'Artillerie… in this towne is wonderfullie decayed,' the court lamented. By then, however, gunpowder had proved its efficacy, allowing archery to evolve into the leisure pursuit we know today.

One man who played a prominent role in that transition, both locally and nationally, was Sir Ashton Lever (1729-88) of Alkrington Hall, Middleton.

Described as the 'father of modern target archery' Lever was a true eccentric, fond of hunting, horse racing at Kersal Moor and the acquisition of small songbirds in large numbers. He also liked to train animals to perform stunts for his guests. Above all he became obsessed with amassing a vast natural history collection, eventually displayed at his own museum in London, set up in Leicester Square in 1774.

Lever took with him to the capital his long-serving and no doubt long suffering secretary and friend, Thomas Waring.

Maybe it was the London air. Maybe it was the hours he sat at his desk in Lever's crowded museum. But at any rate Waring developed health problems and decided to take up archery, a sport he had apparently encountered in his youth.

Waring soon developed a rare passion for the sport. Indeed he almost made a career of it, both as an authority on archery and as a bow maker, a skill he apparently learnt from two of Manchester's many bowyers and fletchers, Edward and John Kelsal of Long Milngate. (The Kelsals' forebears were said to have been amongst the first craftsmen to develop laminated bows, in the late 16th century, in response to the scarcity of suitable yew.)

Not to be outdone, Waring's master soon followed suit in taking up the bow, and with all his usual gusto.

No doubt recalling the images of the Flodden Field longbowmen he had often gazed at in the family church at Middleton (*see right*), in 1777 Sir Ashton and his neighbour, Sir Thomas Egerton of Heaton Hall, established a gentlemen's club named after the Middleton Archers. Lever also helped revive an older association, the Broughton Archers, who met on Kersal Moor (*see p37*).

The majority of these archer revivalists, it must be said, were men of rank, harking after a long-lost ideal of Merrie England, at a time when the first ravages of the industrial revolution were making their presence felt in the hills and valleys around Manchester.

Yet Cheetham Hill was also the home of probably the 18th century's most successful archer, the working-class champion, James Rawson (*see p79*). »

▶ This stained glass segment, at **St Leonard's, Middleton,** no doubt helped stir the imaginations of many a boy in the area, among them quite probably Ashton Lever himself, who was baptised in the church and who lived at nearby Alkrington Hall.

Installed in 1524, the window depicts and names (just above each bow) fifteen of the Middleton longbowmen, as they prayed before the battle of Flodden Field, fought in Northumbria against the Scots in September 1513.

So successful were the archers that their commander, Sir Richard Assheton – grandson of Ralph, the Black Knight – was knighted on the battlefield. As an act of thanksgiving, on his return he rebuilt St Leonard's, commissioned the window and dedicated his flag, helmet, sword and spurs, which may still be seen inside the church.

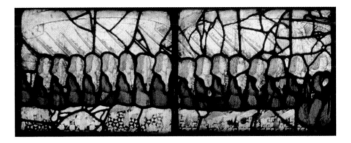

Coincidentally, 240 years later one of Sir Richard's descendants, Mary Assheton of Middleton Hall, stole the heart of Ashton Lever. Given his unruly lifestyle and often unkempt appearance, her father's refusal to sanction the match was no surprise. Lever was nevertheless devastated.

Later still, in 1992, another of Sir Richard's descendants, Lord Clitheroe, became the patron of the newly formed **Assheton Bowmen** (seen below at the ground they share with the North Manchester Rugby Club on Victoria Avenue, Moston). Although a young club, its members are only too aware of their heritage, and are to challenge a Scottish archery club to a friendly return on the 500th anniversary of Flodden Field, in 2013.

Perhaps after the encounter the two sets of archers will repair to the **Middleton Archer** pub, on Kemp Street (which itself is off Archer Park), with its bronze rendition of a bowman by Constance Smith.

▲ **Sir Ashton Lever** of Alkrington Hall wears the flamboyant garb and gold medal of the Royal Toxophilite Society, which he formed in 1780. Lever was one of many aristocrats of the period who fell in love with the romance of archery and its trappings.

Today's target archers must also adhere to a strict dress code, set down by the sport's governing body, the Grand National Archery Society, which formed in 1861. The code states that competitors' uniforms must consist only of white and dark green elements (although this is to be slightly relaxed in 2005 to allow for more distinctive colours).

Shown above right in her white and green kit is a member of the **Eccles Archery Club**, using one of the latest torque resistant 'target recurve bows', made from aluminium and carbon and fitted with a bowsight for greater accuracy. Her arrows are made from carbon fibre.

Some members of the club still use traditional wooden longbows, however, usually made from yew or ash, and still hand-crafted by specialist craftsmen.

The crossbow shown below, made by James Johnson of Market Street Lane, Manchester, c. 1772, is one of some 4,000 archery related artefacts forming the **Simon Archery Collection**, on display at the Manchester Museum, Oxford Road. The crossbow was regarded for many years with suspicion by English bowmen, who thought it a cunning, continental over-elaboration. Crossbows nevertheless become common in rural Lancastrian circles for potting rooks, rabbits and other wildlife. Poachers liked them because they made little noise and because the bolts could be re-used.

Several Manchester gun makers manufactured crossbows until the breach loaded shotgun gained favour in the mid 19th century.

》 Manchester thus emerged as a focal point for archers and archery in the north west.

Back in London, meanwhile, Sir Ashton Lever – knighted in recognition of his natural history collection – was as busy as ever, playing a lead role in the foundation of the influential Toxophilite Society (from Greek *toxon* for bow), in 1780. Based for in Regent's Park and, crucially, patronised by the Prince Regent, the Royal Toxophilites, as they became, made archery firmly fashionable in elite circles.

Even if one could not hit a target, one could cut a dash in one's archery costume.

Each society had its own. The Toxophilites' consisted of a green single-breasted coat with engraved buttons, buff waistcoat, belt, pouch and tassle. The hat had also to sport, Robin Hood-style, at least one green feather.

In a similar vein, James Smith's portrait of Lord Egerton, c. 1783, on display at the Manchester Art Gallery, shows also how aristocrats invested archery with classical, as well as medieval heroic values.

Sport, fashion and myth have thus always been closely intertwined.

Another characteristic of archery was its popularity amongst women (*see also* p18). Indeed by the mid 19th century women actually started to outnumber men at tournaments, particularly once men started to desert archery in favour of the newly fashionable rifle volunteer movement, which, in response to the perceived threat of a French invasion, had 200,000 members by 1861.

Archery then lost out further to the newly popular sports of croquet and lawn tennis as the century wore on. From 130 archery societies in 1881 the total fell to 50 by 1889. According to a letter in *The Field* in 1879, among the casualties were apparently the Broughton Archers and the Cheetham Hill Archers. Nor did the provision of archery ranges at public parks, including Peel Park and Philips Park in 1846, manage to broaden the sport's appeal.

Happily a second and much wider revival ensued during the 20th century, partly owing to its inclusion as an Olympic sport, so that today some 1100 clubs are affiliated to the Grand National Archery Society.

And in Manchester, feathered hats may no longer be obligatory, but Sir Ashton's spirit does linger on in one other respect.

Ingo Simon (1875-1964), whose father established the Simon Engineering Group in Stockport, was a leading archer whose 1914 flight-shot, measuring 462 yards, remained a world record until 1933. Simon's wife Erna was herself world champion in 1937.

In 1955 Simon became the president of the Royal Toxophilite Society (which by then had moved to Burnham in Berkshire). The following year he was appointed the first president of the Society of Archer Antiquaries.

He was the obvious choice, because in common with Sir Ashton, Ingo and Erna Simons' passion was collecting; not in the field of natural history but archaeological and ethnographic material related to archery, gathered from their travels around the world and donated, in 1946, to the Manchester Museum, where the collection may now be viewed in a modern gallery setting.

Sir Ashton, one feels sure, would have heartily approved.

▲ It was not only the gentry who took up the bow in the 18th century. **James Rawson** of Cheetham Hill, whose unsigned portrait hangs in the headquarters of the Royal Toxophilite Society in Burnham, Berkshire, was reputedly the best archer in Britain.

According to a contemporary, Thomas Roberts, author of *The English Bowman*, Rawson was 'a stout middle-sized man, and being a man's shoe-maker by trade; had (in the exercise of the business) increased the force, and hardened the muscles of his arms to such a degree that his power over the bow was exceedingly great.'

Roberts went on to report that Rawson claimed in front of Thomas Waring that he had once shot an arrow 'eighteen score yards' (that is, 360 yards, or 329m), albeit on slightly declining ground. Although no official record of the shot existed, Roberts refused to disbelieve Rawson. Indeed, he noted that a member of the Royal Toxophilites had shot 340 yards, measured and witnessed, and that Rawson's 'back'd-bow' (that is, reinforced with two types of wood in tension) would have been more powerful.

If true, no modern archer using a similar bow has been able to match Rawson. On the other hand, it could it have been that as a relatively short man, Rawson's paces were not quite a full yard.

Whatever, one other factor that separated Rawson from Sir Ashton Lever, Thomas Waring and their ilk, was that Rawson was a professional, a working-class champion – the 'Lancashire Tell' no less – earning his living by travelling the country, challenging all-comers and profiting from side bets.

As the inscription on his grave proclaims:

Here were deposited the Earthly remains of James Rawson who died Oct 1st 1795 Aged 80 Years.
His dexterity as an Archer was unrivaled. From the age of 16 to 60 he never refused a challenge, nor ever lost a Match.
Grim death grown jealous of his art,
His matchless fame to stop,
Relentless aim'd th'unerring dart,
And split the Vital Prop.
This favourite Son Apollo eyed,
His Virtues to requite,
Convey'd his Spirit to reside,
In beams of endless Light.

Unfortunately Rawson's grave lies abandoned and inaccessible to the public in the fenced-off, overgrown churchyard of what was once St Mark's Church, on St Mark's Lane, Cheetham Hill.

The church – demolished in the 1990s – had been built a year before Rawson's death, coincidentally on the very ground where Rawson and the Cheetham Hill archers had once gathered.

Next to this ground was a pub, the Shooting Butt Inn, until this too was demolished to make way for the late Victorian pub which still stands on the site.

It's name? The Robin Hood, naturally.

Chapter Ten

Bowls

The sign of the Bowling Green Hotel, Brookburn Road, Chorlton-cum-Hardy. The current building dates from 1908, though its adjoining green is thought to have been laid when the original pub was built c.1780.

It is often said that there is no scene more quintessentially English than that of a cricket match being played on a village green on a balmy summer's day.

But there is, at least in sporting and historical terms.

For cricket is a relative newcomer when compared to bowls, and not only in English villages. Southampton and Chesterfield believe their bowling greens date back to the 13th century. Hereford claims theirs was laid in 1484.

During the 16th and 17th centuries bowls was *the* national game. Sir Francis Drake we know about. But kings and labourers, nuns and wives played too (Mrs Pepys among them). Even John Knox and John Calvin liked the odd game, on Sundays no less.

But bowls today is no mere quaint survival. Nearly 600,000 players, male and female, make it Britain's fifth most popular competitive sport. Manchester alone has over 300 clubs. As the 1923 *British Bowls Annual* noted, 'The Lancashire man turns to bowls as ducks go to the water.'

The first reference to a bowling green in Manchester appeared in James Ogden's *A Description of Manchester*, in 1783. Walking eastwards from Castlefield Ogden crossed the River Tib 'near the bowling green'. A map of 1794 showed a 'new bowling green' near Strangeways Hall, while in the early 19th century the sole recreation of the scientist John Dalton was to play bowls every Thursday at the Dog and Partridge Inn on Chester Road, Old Trafford (demolished in 2001).

The first set of modern rules for the game, drafted by a Glasgow solicitor, appeared in 1849. A later set was published by George and Thomas Royle, Bowl Makers of Tib Street, Manchester, on behalf of Broughton Cricket Club, in 1868.

But what really restored bowls to its pre-eminent place in the hearts of British sportsmen and women was urbanisation. As more fields and common land succumbed to development, bowling greens turned out to be the right size to slot into the emerging pattern of streets and houses. Unlike football or cricket

grounds they were compact, and were used, daytime and evening, for up to six months a year.

To play you did not have to be fit, or own special gear. Nor did bowls eat up too much of a working man's precious free time.

But perhaps best of all – just like billiards, which would achieve similar popularity between the 1870s and the 1930s – on a bowling green one could have a smoke, a pint, a bet and a match, all at the same time. Small wonder the breweries loved the game and laid down greens wherever they could in the growing suburbs of Withington and Fallowfield, Broughton and Prestwich.

Every class of Mancunian found a place to bowl. For the aspiring middle classes there were clubs like the Old Trafford Bowling Club, formed in 1877. Cricket clubs, and after the 1880s, tennis clubs, adopted bowls eagerly too. Indeed, once a cricketer's knees had gone he would be ceremonially presented with a pair of woods and inducted seamlessly into the bowls section. Thus he could remain active, and the club

Bowling Green, Alexandra Park, Moss Side.

◄ Manchester's first municipal bowling green, shown here in 1910, was laid out at **Alexandra Park**, shortly after the park opened in 1871. Seen today from the same viewpoint (*above*), the bowls pavilion on the right, backing onto Smalldale Avenue, no longer exists, although the outline of the sunken green can still be discerned, as can the original stone steps. Beyond the green and now in a dilapidated state amid the trees, is the original park lodge, by Alfred Darbyshire.

Alexandra Park itself was designed by Alexander Hennell and was highly regarded for its innovative layout and use of ornamentation. Separate play-grounds, or 'gymnasia' were provided for boys and girls, plus a cricket oval, later converted into tennis courts, and a putting green, with a bandstand in the centre. In 1934 an outdoor swimming pool was added, south of the green (*see p121*).

Alexandra Park is now a Grade II registered landscape.

could count on receiving his subs for many years to follow.

Yet for all its popularity, the formal organisation of bowls came relatively late, and when it did occur, in 1903, it resulted in a schism within the bowls world that remains as clear and distinct today as it was over a century ago.

Just as rugby split into Union and League in 1895, so too did bowls split into two distinct regional camps; crown green, mainly in the industrial north – from the Trent to the Ribble, as was often said – and flat green (also known as lawn or rink bowls) in the south and far north.

Manchester, needless to add, was and remains crown green to the core.

How the two codes differ is both a simple and a complex matter. Apart from subtle variations in the rules, flat green bowlers, under the aegis of English Bowls Association (formed by the cricketing legend, WG Grace), wear whites and tend to refinement and decorum. Their greens are, of course, as flat as flat can reasonably be.

Crown green bowlers dress informally, behave informally, like a bet, make a noise and play on greens which typically rise in the centre between 9 and 15 inches.

Crown green bowlers play any which way across the green, taking advantage of its mounds and dips. Flat green bowlers play in strictly divided sectors, called rinks.

For crown green bowlers their spiritual home is Blackpool; for flat green it is Worthing.

But crown green or flat green, there is serious concern for the future of bowls in the context of our national heritage. Since the 1950s, hundreds of greens have been built on by developers, or in the case of pubs, turned into car parks. In the ten years leading up to 2004, 23 clubs or greens were lost in the Altrincham area alone.

Parks greens are also in decline. Whereas Manchester maintained 71 municipal greens in 1927, now it manages only 31.

Bowls, in one form or another, has been played in Britain for at least 800 years. Several of our greens are amongst the oldest sports grounds still in use, anywhere in the world.

And by 2023, we are told, 30 per cent of the population will be aged over 60.

In short, the bowling greens of Britain are no mere sporting curiosities. These precious green oases in the midst of our towns and cities are part of our wider heritage. They represent continuity, and perhaps even a small token of hope for our future health as a nation.

If that is not quintessential, then what is?

▲ **Premier Bowls** of Hollands Mill, Stockport, is one of a handful of specialist suppliers still working with wood. For around 350 years, until the introduction of composite, or synthetic materials, in 1931, bowls, or 'woods', were manufactured almost exclusively from lignum vitae, the 'wood of life', so-called because of its medicinal properties. (In the 16th century it was thought, wrongly, to cure syphilis.) Imported mainly from the Caribbean, lignum vitae is the hardest, densest wood known to man. Because of its high fat and resin content it is also self-lubricating and virtually impervious to water. Over the centuries it has therefore proved ideal for bowls (and ship's propellors, Mosquito aircraft, chisel handles, gavels... the list is long.)

Nowadays the import of lignum-vitae is strictly controlled, which means that surplus woods are snapped up for re-cycling. Not only is this environmentally laudable; it is also a happy by-product of one of the differences that exists between flat green and crown green bowling.

The standard bowl for the former weighs 3lbs or more and is larger than its crown green counterpart, which usually weighs between 2lbs 4 ounces and 2lbs 14 ounces.

It is therefore possible for Premier Bowls to take an unwanted flat green bowl and, by reducing it on a lathe, turn it into a shiny, desirable wood for a crown green bowler to enjoy for many years to come. Some lignum vitae bowls still in use, it is thought, are over a century old, such is the wood's extraordinary durability.

That longevity is one explanation why so many spares can still be found. Another is that flat green bowlers use four balls, whereas crown green players need only two. But the main reason for the surplus is that all flat green bowlers have now gone over to composites, whereas, Premier Bowls estimate, one fifth of all crown green players still prefer the feel, warmth and performance of woods.

One crucial characteristic of all bowls is their bias. This makes them roll in a curved trajectory as they slow down, and is governed by their slightly ovoid shape.

Some of Premier Bowls equipment originated from George and Thomas Royle, Bowl Makers, whose premises in 1868 were in Tib Street, Manchester.

▲ Shown here are three of the Manchester area's oldest private bowling clubs, each with its own tale of struggle. The **Lloyds BC** (*above*), attached to the late 19th century Lloyd's Hotel, Chorlton, is a success story. Its green, originally laid in 1870, was saved in 2002 when, after a vigorous campaign backed by local MP Keith Bradley and by Manchester City Council, the Lees brewery granted the club a 25 year lease at the modest rental of £150 per annum. There has been a price to pay. Four-storey blocks of flats built on the pub's former car park and on an adjacent plot, formerly a tennis court, will now overlook the green. On the other hand, the flats' presence will improve security for the club.

In Altrincham, the green of the **Stamford BC** (*right*) dates back to at least 1844 and is in the heart of a conservation area. But in 2004 the green's new owner gave the club notice to quit unless it paid an annual rent of £5,000. Previously the club's mainly elderly members paid no rent. Two earlier attempts by developers to build on the green in 2001 were blocked by Trafford MBC, following a concerted campaign by bowlers, residents and the local MP, Graham Brady. But now the club has been shut out, the future of yet another historic open space is once again in grave doubt.

For the **Old Trafford BC**, Talbot Road (*above*), the pressure comes not from developers but from the onerous legacy of the club's founders. The land on which they settled in 1877 was part of the Trafford Park estate. To the north lay the Botanical Gardens (*see Chapter 2*). To the south, from 1881-1908, was the Northern Tennis Club. The green itself once formed a corner of the Manchester Cricket Club ground, and until the 1960s was bordered by detached villas. Now it is surrounded by offices and retail outlets.

Most bowls clubs manage to make do with modest pavilions. But the founders of Old Trafford BC – who included various merchants (cotton, timber, cigars), a tallow chandler, a jeweller, and indeed the manager of the Manchester Cricket Club, but certainly no wealthy patrons as would be the case, for example, at the Manchester Tennis and Racquet Club (*see p86*) – erected in 1877 what was at the time one of the most substantial clubhouses in amateur sport.

Maintaining the fabric of this classic Tudorbethan pavilion places a continual strain on the club. Added to which, in 2003 it spent £14,000 on the green alone.

But in one respect the club is blessed – by its neighbours, Lancashire CCC and Manchester United, or at least by their fans, who pay handsomely to park in the club's car park on match days.

Without this income, life at this, the least known of Old Trafford's sporting treasures, would be quite, quite different.

▲ The **Wythenshawe Park Bowls and Tennis Pavilion**, by the City of Manchester Architect, Leonard C Howitt, opened c.1960, is a rare example of a parks pavilion designed in a modernist style. Its stripped upper storey has a balcony, club room and changing facilities, supported by a free-standing circular pier. Best known for his Hollins College (otherwise called the 'Toastrack'), Howitt also designed the Sharston swimming baths *(see p126)*, opened in 1961.

Wythenshawe's green is of course designed for crown green bowling. But thanks to the 2002 Commonwealth Games, Manchester now has a flat green facility too, a rarity indeed in Lancashire (though others might call it an alien intrusion.)

The admirable £1 million bowls centre at **Heaton Park** (*above right*) – built in 2001 as part of a £32.2 million Lottery and Council funded restoration programme currently under way in the park – serves two local flat green clubs and has four slightly sunken and neatly edged greens. Overlooking these is an simply articulated pavilion, designed by McBains Cooper, which uses glazed panels and varied finishes to create a refreshingly light, airy but also welcoming atmosphere. Certainly since hosting the 2002 Games, the pavilion and the now-maturing greens have done much to raise flat green's profile in the north west. Apart from staging regional finals, it is hoped Heaton Park will also host the prestigious British Isles Championships, in 2008.

One of the most troubling issues affecting parks greens, not only in Manchester, is the common misuse of greens by wilful passers-by (dog owners especially). Since the mid 1990s therefore every green in Manchester's parks – Wythenshawe excepted – has had to be surrounded by anti-vandal palisade fences, as at the David Lewis Recreation Ground (*above*), in Boggart Hole Clough, Blackley. In time the local authority, which has also set up a Bowling Green Council to discuss the bowlers' ongoing concerns, hopes to instal less obtrusive fences. But it is a grim reflection on modern life that they are necessary at all.

▶ A fine summer's evening at the **Grange Club**, Edgeley Road, Stockport, one of hundreds of private greens in the Manchester area where, hidden behind hedges or tucked at the rear of pubs or working men's clubs, old friends gather to enjoy this most ancient, and gentlest of sports.

Or at least that is how it may seem. In reality, a crown green bowls tournament is full of ribald comment and rivalry. This is, after all, a gathering of experts. Many of the onlookers are players themselves, who know every inch of the green; its idiosyncracies, soft spots and seasonal variations. More than likely they will also have played against some of the bowlers out on the turf.

Like all sub-cultures, crown green has a language, a humour and a rhythm of its own. A bowler will play 'up to the knob' or set up a 'bobby'. Cries of 'big yard!' 'get on!' or 'peg hard!' echo across the green. From the omnipresent bookies one hears the constant whisper of odds and upsets.

Unlike their flat green counterparts, crown green 'trundlers' have never had the least compunction about playing for money. Indeed during the early 20th century the top five or six crown green bowlers, most of them Lancastrians, earned up to £40 a week, making them by far the best paid sportsmen in the

country. (A footballer's maximum wage was £4 by comparison.)

But not all runs smoothly in the world of crown green bowling.

For whereas it is possible to go flat green bowling in all weathers, in one of the many indoor centres now operating around Britain, by the very nature of its surface, crown green cannot be easily be tamed for modern convenience. And whereas crown green is played

only in select areas of England, flat green is played all over the world. There was therefore no place for crown green at the Commonwealth Games, simply because there is no international competition to be had.

Flat green has also shown itself ready to embrace modernity.

To spice up the sport's televisual appeal, team members are kitted out in stylised sportsgear and play with coloured bowls, while

even the artificial mats used for indoor competitions are no longer automatically green.

Not that any of this distant folly intrudes upon a summer evening's play at the Grange or at Boggart Hole Clough.

Yet such scenes cannot and should not be taken for granted.

For if they are, they will surely be lost to indifference, if not to bricks and mortar.

Chapter Eleven

Real Tennis

The badge of the Manchester Tennis and Racquet Club shows the two main games played at its Salford headquarters. Both games have variable nomenclatures. The round headed 'racket' – note the different spelling – is for the game of 'racquets', which is often also written as 'rackets' (though seldom as 'racquet' as in the title of the Manchester club). The other racket is for the game of 'real tennis', which is also often referred to as 'royal tennis', or even as plain 'tennis', to distinguish it from lawn tennis. Squash and skittles are also on offer at the club.

A short stroll from Deansgate lies one of the city's most important yet least known bastions of sporting heritage, the Manchester Tennis and Racquet Club on Blackfriars Road, Salford.

The tennis played there is not tennis as we know it, but 'real tennis', one of Britain's oldest sports; from which squash, fives, racquets and that Victorian upstart, lawn tennis, all evolved.

Manchester's club, which formed in 1874 and moved to its current headquarters six years later, is one of just 24 real tennis clubs operating in Britain today, compared with nearly a hundred known to have been active before 1914. Yet in real tennis terms, it is a relative newcomer.

The world's oldest court still in use, at Falkland Palace, Fife, dates from 1539 and is open air. The better known one at Hampton Court – also still active and the model on which all subsequent indoor designs were based – was built in 1625.

To see the game's eccentrically designed courts, to hear its obscure terminology, even to handle the solid, handmade balls, is to understand just how tenaciously real tennis has clung to tradition.

There has been one radical departure however. The use of rackets, starting in the 15th century, was at first derided in France, where the game originated, and where it was played with the hands only, under the title *jeu de paume*.

By that time the game had spread to England, where the name 'tennis' arose from the old French command *tenetz!* or 'take this!' shouted by the server.

Shakespeare made several allusions to tennis. In *Much Ado About Nothing*, for example, Claudio implies that unscrupulous court professionals – *maître paumiers* – used human hair to stuff tennis balls. When Samuel Pepys saw Charles II play at Whitehall he cringed at the 'loathsome' flattery of fawning onlookers.

Courts for 'royal' tennis now became almost as *de rigueur* amongst the English gentry as bowling greens had been in the 17th century. London, Oxford and Cambridge gained new ones, modelled on Hampton Court. In the north west the first is thought to have been in Liverpool, in 1750.

But being indoors and subject to hard wear, real tennis courts were expensive to build and maintain. In addition to which, in the 1870s a new sport emerged that would ultimately overshadow the old game completely. Lawn tennis.

Nevertheless, 20 real tennis courts opened between 1870-1914, including Manchester (1880), Newcastle (1894), Moreton Morrell, in Warwickshire (1905), and in London, the Queen's Club (1888) and Lord's (1900), both designed by WC Marshall, an early member at Manchester.

This period also saw the introduction of a new form of floor and wall rendering, reportedly more durable and stable in humid conditions. The builder responsible, Joseph Bickley, is said to have taken the secret of his formula to the grave.

In common with most of its contemporaries, the Manchester Tennis and Racquet Club was always more then a sports club.

For years its central location and well-stocked cellars made it a popular haunt for bishops, MPs and, among many leading businessmen, Edgar Baerlein, a fine amateur player of both types of tennis. The city's rugby union elite often dropped by for lunch before a game, while the club's proximity to Castle Irwell made it a favourite with the racing fraternity.

Women, typically in such sporting circles, were not admitted as members until 1980.

Also a regular at Blackfriars Road was the legendary all-rounder Max Woosnam, who played football for Manchester City and lawn tennis at the Northern.

But Manchester's finest was Peter Latham, who started work at the club's original Miller Street premises in 1876, aged 11, and rose to become world racquets champion from 1887-1902, and world real tennis champion from 1895-1905, by which time he had moved to become the professional at the Queen's Club in London.

The Queen's Club, incidentally, remains the home of the sport's governing body, which also has jurisdiction over racquets (a game developed during the 18th century in London's prisons, of all places, where inmates played it against the tall perimeter walls).

Nowadays membership at Blackfriars Road stands at around 400, and the club remains an important hub in what is a vibrant national scene. For example three real tennis clubs have opened since 1998, at Bristol, Prested Hall (Essex) and Hendon (London).

The sport is thus a remarkable survivor, and although some of its adherents decry the prefix 'real' – arguing that it is 'tennis' pure and simple – both the game's ethos and spirit are very real indeed.

◀ An unlikely and little known gem, the Grade II* listed **Manchester Tennis and Racquet Club** on Blackfriars Road, Salford, was designed by George T Redmayne (a pupil of Alfred Waterhouse) and opened in 1880. It is one of 24 real tennis clubs functioning in England (nine of which are listed).

Other than the club's name in terracotta mouldings above the main entrance, the exterior is relatively anonymous. Yet, as revealed overleaf, the interior is rich in period detail.

Above the original two storeys of the main entrance is a fives court, added in 1926. The court's glazed roof can be seen in the aerial view, running at a right angle to the roofs of both the real tennis court (at the rear) and the smaller racquet court (nearest Blackfriars Road).

The club forms part of a interesting enclave of Victorian institutional buildings. Immediately adjoining the club is the former Blackfriars Baths (b. 1879-80), now converted into storage space. Its chimney is visible next to the club's end wall. Adjacent to this is the former Sacred Trinity School (1891-92), which itself is next to the former Mission House and Clergy House of Sacred Trinity (1898). On nearby Collier Street is another Grade II* building, the Greengate Baths (see page 117).

▶ The layout, if not the structure of Manchester's real tennis court, is virtually identical to that of Hampton Court (built 1625). Three sides feature sloping projections, called the *penthouse*, thought to represent church buttresses. On the *hazard* side, an added projection (seen in the far right corner) is called the *tambour*. On the left, the *galleries* resemble cloister openings, while behind the receiver's end, the *grille* (visible above the net on the right) has been likened to a buttery hatch.

Each of these curious projections and voids plays a part in the game's tactics and arcane scoring system. So too do the all-important grid-like floor markings, used to score what is called a *chase*.

The rackets are smaller than for lawn tennis, while the balls, formed from solid cores wrapped tightly with cloth, hardly bounce at all. This explains why the game must be played on a hard surface (and why tennis on grass only became possible once air-filled rubber balls were invented in the 1860s).

One drawback of real tennis is that relatively few spectators are able to watch. At Manchester, as at most clubs, viewing is mainly from behind the *dedans* (from where this photograph was taken), in a narrow, low-ceilinged area in which 40-50 onlookers can peer through the opening, protected by netting.

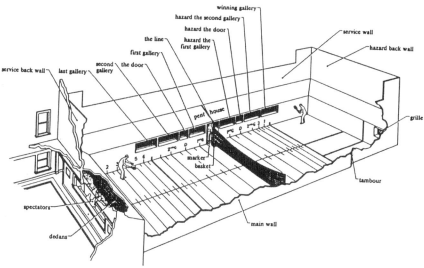

▲ Little changed in over a century, the Manchester Tennis and Racquet Club's entrance hall, changing rooms, bathroom and original skittles alley show why the building has been granted Grade II* listed status. There used to be an inter-connecting door between the dressing rooms (*above*) and the Blackfriars Road swimming baths. Note the small seat at the back of the skittles alley (*above right*). This was for the alley boy to perch on so that he could return the solid lignum vitae wooden bowls – many of which are still in use today – and stand up the skittles for the next bowler. Also on the premises is a workshop for the club professional who, in addition to his coaching duties, just like the *maitre paumiers* of medieval Paris, makes all the club's balls by hand and re-strings rackets when required.

Chapter Twelve

Lacrosse

Lacrosse action from a Manchester Waconians v. Cheadle match at the Didsbury Cricket Club, where lacrosse has been played for over a century. The Waconians, who field eight teams, from under-12s to seniors, were relative latecomers to the lacrosse scene when formed in 1911 by old boys from the Manchester Warehousemen & Clerks' Orphans School (later Cheadle Hulme Grammar School). Cheadle, in green and gold, formed in 1879 and have won more Northern Flags Finals over the last 25 years than any other club.

Historians often have difficulty explaining why certain sports, such as crown green bowls or rugby league, took root in one part of the country yet not another. Lacrosse is one such sport.

Its origins are in north America, where for centuries tribal teams, often made up of hundreds if not thousands of participants, played this ancient ball game fast and furiously across great distances. French settlers in the 17th century noted that the strangely formed sticks used in the game resembled a bishop's crozier, or 'crosse'.

Not until 1867, in Montreal, was La Crosse codified for European consumption. That same year the first of many exhibition tours undertaken by Canadian teams to venues across the USA, Britain, France and Ireland took place.

Five lacrosse clubs started up in England as a result; at Blackheath, Richmond, Sheffield and, in Manchester, at Old Trafford cricket ground, and at Broughton Cricket Club.

A second, more commercial tour by teams of white Canadians and American Indians – the latter playing in war paint and feathers – followed in 1876 and led to the formation of further clubs in London, Liverpool, Glasgow, Dublin and Belfast. Yet while all these would eventually disband, at least five of the new clubs formed in the Manchester area not only survived but thrived. These included Stockport, whose founders came across the game purely by chance (*see* p92).

A third exhibition tour, in 1883, took two more Canadian teams upon a gruelling 12 week tour involving at least 42 matches in 35 different towns and cities (roughly one match every two days). But as the *Boys Own Paper* reported, 'Britons are proverbially conservative in their pastimes, and it is not easy... to attract paying patronage to what is, to most people, a new and strange game.'

Perhaps so, but again, not in and around Manchester, where three tour games were staged, plus one in Rochdale, and where the game continued to gain favour.

A North of England Lacrosse Association was formed as early as 1879, and by 1909 there were said to be around 100 lacrosse teams playing every week in Lancashire and Cheshire.

A surprising number of them, moreover, still exist.

Of the twelve English clubs formed prior to 1900 that still operate today, ten are from the north west. Only the lacrosse clubs of Hampstead, in London, and Cambridge University, both formed in 1882, are as old.

Of the 115 or so lacrosse clubs currently affiliated to the English Lacrosse Assocation – itself based in Manchester – a quarter are from Lancashire and Cheshire.

In men's lacrosse particularly, Manchester and Stockport clubs dominate.

Why this should be so is hard to fathom. Is there perhaps something in the winter air, or in the softness of the turf, or in the blood of the people, that lends this most poised and disciplined of ball games to this one region of England? Or is it due solely to the energy of the pioneers? English lacrosse has always been an amateur game played by elite schools and universities. But such institutions are hardly confined to Manchester and Stockport.

Whatever the explanation for this curious phenomenon, for the record the region's venerable clubs are: Stockport (formed 1876 and thus the world's oldest surviving lacrosse club), Cheadle (1879), Heaton Mersey (1879), Manchester University (formed as Owen's College, 1883), Oldham and Werneth (1883), William Hulme's Grammar School (1887), Rochdale (1888), Poynton (formed as Offerton, 1889), Timperley (formed as Chorlton, 1891), Cheadle Hulme (1893), Hulmeians (1893), Ashton (1896), Boardman and Eccles (named after Boardman Street, 1906), Heaton Mersey Guild (1907), Norbury (formed as Disley, 1908), Old Waconians (1911) and Mellor (1925).

Despite their longevity, none of these clubs owns its own ground. Instead, playing in winter, they happily share with other sports clubs, mainly cricket.

But sporting heritage should never be measured solely in terms of bricks and mortar.

The contribution of lacrosse clubs to the character of the local sporting scene runs deeper than that, and should be a measure of no small pride.

◄ Reflecting the customs of the north American Indians who invented the game, the winners of lacrosse finals traditionally have their names embroidered on a decorative banner. Pictured here is the Northern Association Challenge Flag for the period 1890-98. Roughly one metre in width, it takes pride of place above the bar of the Cale Green pavilion, Stockport.

Amongst the club names which can just be made out on either side of the standing figures (themselves unidentifiable), are South Manchester (since defunct), winners in 1890, 1891, 1892 and 1895, and Cheetham, winners in 1893 and 1894.

Stockport Lacrosse Club retained the flag having won the Finals in 1896, 1897 and 1898. They went on to win the competition every year thereafter until 1903, and for three further years in a row from 1910-13.

The flag shown here is not the oldest in English lacrosse however.

The one awarded for the first six Flags Finals, dating from 1884-89, hangs in the bar of Didsbury Cricket Club, Wilmslow Road, which is shared with the Manchester Waconians club.

Another competition in men's lacrosse is the Iroquois Cup, played annually between the winners of the Northern and Southern Flags Finals. Since this was first contested in 1896, southern clubs have won the cup on only six occasions, and not once since 1976.

▲ **Cale Green** pavilion, Stockport
– c.1894 with an extension (*left*)
added 1930 – is the centrepiece
of an eleven acre ground owned
jointly by the **Stockport Lacrosse
Club** (the oldest lacrosse club
in the world) and the **Stockport
Cricket and Bowls Club** (formed by
gentlemen of the town in 1855). A
feature of the pavilion rarely seen
now are two gates leading onto the
pitch; one for amateur cricketers,
one for professionals. It was the
same at Lord's and many other
grounds until well into the 20th
century.

Cale Green is also unusual for
having its own war memorial. But
the reason for featuring Cale Green
here is its association with lacrosse.

Although Stockport Lacrosse
Club have played at other grounds
during their long history, Cale Green
is their true home. Currently they
field four men's, four boys', two

ladies' and four girls' teams, all
run by volunteers. Cale Green was
also for many years the venue for
lacrosse's leading mens' event, the
Northern Flags Final.

On occasions these and other
major matches at Cale Green have
attracted crowds of up to 3-4,000
spectators bunched around the
lacrosse pitch, which lies to the
west of the cricket circle. (More
recent finals have been staged at
Brooklands and Rochdale.)

Often told is the story of how
Stockport Lacrosse Club was born.

Apparently certain former
members of the Stockport Rugby
Club – recently disbanded after
a player's death during a match
– were returning to Stockport one
afternoon in April 1876 when their
train halted at signals. Looking
down onto the Longsight Cricket
Ground (since built over) they
caught a glimpse of an exhibition

match being played between the
Canadian Montreal Club and the
Caughnawaga Indians.

Intrigued – as everyone is, seeing
lacrosse for the first time – they
agreed to try it out. For their first six
years, playing at Shaw Heath, then
at the old Stockport Cricket Ground
in Charles Street, the Stockport
players were hopeless. But they
improved thereafter and between
1895 and the 1930s dominated
the sport. More recently they also
won the Final in 2004, thus adding
another flag to the collection lining
the pavilion walls at Cale Green.

One of the crowd at Longsight
in 1876 was Norman Melland,
a famous Mancunian all-rounder
who later played for Stockport and
Owens College. Melland wrote two
seminal books on lacrosse, excelled
at tennis, billiards and hockey, and
was a co-founder of the Manchester
Ice Palace (*see p97*).

▲ The family firm of TS Hattersley and Son Ltd – based at the Lacrosse Works, Weymouth Road, Eccles, since 1965 – is one of only two companies in the world making wooden lacrosse sticks, or 'crosses' (the other being on an Indian reservation near Buffalo, USA).

Hattersley's started out in the 1870s making cricket bats, then tennis rackets, at its original works in Gilda Brook Road, Eccles.

But as lacrosse became increasingly popular, particularly at girls' schools, the company started making their own crosses in the early 1900s.

Most male players use synthetic sticks nowadays. But the wooden variety (*left*) remains popular with girls and women. They are still crafted in the traditional way from American white hickory and finished with a bag or net made from leather laces and synthetic cord. Ironically, many of Hattersley's crosses are exported back to north America. They are also now sold in Japan.

Chapter Thirteen

Skating

In the days before climate change had us basking in January and shivering in July, when our ponds and waterways would regularly freeze for days if not weeks on end most winters, Britain's skaters had ample opportunity to take to the ice, by necessity if not for pleasure.

James Drake Digby, founder of the National Skating Association, wrote in 1893 that lovers of 'glacial sports' in the Metropolis – who at one time included Victoria and Albert – could expect, on average, 15 days of skating and curling per year. In earlier centuries the freezes lasted longer; 14 weeks in 1410 being just one example. In 1819 the Thames at Lambeth froze to a depth of 12 feet from November to March.

In the Manchester area a number of rivers, lakes and ponds are known to have been popular with skaters; the artificial lakes at Heaton Park, Belle Vue and Philips Park, and the curling pond at Old Trafford, for example. In Chorlton-cum-Hardy a large field behind Brookburn Road was deliberately flooded for the benefit of local skaters.

Britain's first skating club is thought to have formed in Edinburgh, possibly as early as 1642. Members of the Royal Toxopholite Society (*see Archery*) formed a club at Regent's Park in 1830, while out in the Fens, crowds of up to 10,000 would gather along ice-bound canals to bet on speed skating races between farm labourers. Two of the fastest were nicknamed 'Gutta Percha' and 'Turkey'.

Fairweather skating at a number of newly created roller rinks, meanwhile, became possible in the 1870s thanks to the arrival of the first modern roller skates from America in 1863, and the development of an improved type of asphalt surfacing.

'Rincomania', as the new craze was called, had arrived.

But for some, this wheel-bound novelty was not enough.

Several attempts were made to create a substitute for ice. The first, in Baker Street, London, in 1841, offered skaters a surface of crystallised alum, hog's lard, soda salt and melted sulphur. It apparently felt like hardened

cheese, smelt awful, and falling over on it was not advised.

Several false starts later, the first breakthrough was made in London in 1870. Professor, John Gamgee, who that same year was also credited with inventing the slot machine, took out a patent for a new type of refrigeration process. His principal aim had been to find a safe method for freezing meat being shipped from Australia to Britain. But keen to capitalise on 'rincomania', in 1874 he turned his thoughts to skating.

Finally, on January 7 1876, the world's first operational, man-made ice rink was unveiled.

Measuring just 24 x 16 feet, Gamgee's 'Glacarium' was on the Kings Road, Chelsea, in a canvas-lined shed. 'Noblemen, gentlemen and ladies only' were admitted. But the press loved it. Safer than asphalt, pronounced *The Lancet*. 'Rollers are child's play after real skates,' declared *The Standard*.

Within weeks Gamgee replaced this first Glacarium with a second improved version measuring 40 x 21 feet, complete with Alpine decor and orchestra

Rusholme's Glacarium (*right*) sketched for the *Illustrated Sporting and Dramatic News* in January 1877. As two rival technologies – asphalt and ice – battled it out for customers, *Punch* delivered its verdict in a verse entitled 'Gamgee to Celia':

Rink with me on Nature's ice, and I'll match hers with mine;
Out of your asphaltes, so cracked up, 'tis I will take the shine.
I make an ice that's more than nice – ethereal, divine!
And they in Rinks that would invest, had best buy into mine.

gallery. But would it survive the summer? August 9 1876 was one of the hottest days ever known in London. To widespread acclaim, the ice survived. 'There is,' predicted the *Illustrated Sporting and Dramatic News*, 'a brilliant future for Glacaria.'

Within months a third London rink opened, inside a swimming pool at Charing Cross. But outside London, surprisingly, only one taker emerged.

Manchester's business community in the 19th century, we know, was hardly risk averse, and was also no doubt keenly attuned to the possibilities of the burgeoning commercial leisure market, and to the notion of science as an economic driver.

But to build Britain's first Glacarium out of London in, of all places, a back street of Rusholme?

One explanation is that Gamgee's brother, Sam, was a professor at nearby Owens College, and that he may have been instrumental in finding the site – the grounds of private house on Moor Street (now Whitecliff Close). Another is the promise of healthy custom from the gated enclave of nearby Victoria Park.

Whatever, the world's fourth, and largest Glacarium, 112 x 36 feet, cost at least £20,000, with no guarantee of success. Its refrigeration unit was imported from Geneva, its boilers, tubes and tanks came from Galloways of Manchester and Hydes & Bennett of Sheffield. WH Beck of London was the engineer, a Mr Hull from Manchester the architect.

Opened with a gala event on January 9 1877, the Rusholme Glacarium was an immediate success. Despite an entrance fee of 2s 6d – set high both to recoup costs and attract an exclusive clientele – it was often busy, with up to a hundred skaters at any one time. Abel Heywood, the Mayor (who knew more about public taste than most having made his fortune selling 'penny dreadfuls') considered it 'one of the grandest illustrations of the progress of science it was possible to conceive.'

The *Daily News* added that 'in comparison with asphalte... not only is the labour of skating infinitely less than the violent propulsions necessary on wheels, but the cool temperature refreshes the skater during the whole period of his exercise.' »

This sumptuous quilted satin skating jacket (from the Platt Hall Gallery of Costume) dates from the same decade as Gamgee's Glacaria. Tennis and archery were also popular among women, but skating had the advantage of being non-competitive and balletic. Rinks also provided tantalising opportunities for men to offer female skaters a helping hand or a supporting arm.

The uniquely Scottish sport of curling at the Rusholme Glacarium, as illustrated in the *The Looking Glass* magazine of February 1 1878. Many of these bearded gentlemen might also have been regulars at the outdoor curling pond at Old Trafford, where Sir Humphrey de Trafford liked to play, or on the lake at Belle Vue, where curling was first offered in the 1890s.

A second bout of 'rincomania' at the turn of the 20th century led to the construction of at least 450 roller skating rinks across Britain, this time with maple instead of asphalt flooring. They included the apparently luxurious Imperial at Ardwick, depicted above in 1904, plus the Palace (Stretford Road), Olympia (Rusholme), Belle Vue, Empress Hall (Cheetham Hill), White City (Old Trafford), De Luxe (Sale) and Whitworth Park. There was even a short-lived Manchester & District Roller Hockey League. The boom did not last however, and by the 1930s most of the city's rinks had closed.

>> A local reporter went further. 'It is scarcely possible to think of anything more ludicrous than skating on real ice in July, and yet we shall all be able to do this ludicrous thing because a scientific gentleman has wisely applied his knowledge to the study of our amusement.'

Alas, by July the Glacarium had closed. And although it did re-open – after a well 113 feet deep was dug in order to tap cooler water – its technical problems persisted. Inside the building the atmosphere apparently grew mistier and more uncomfortable, while running costs were proving ruinously expensive.

This was hardly surprising considering the complexity of Gamgee's method.

The surface alone consisted of a six inch concrete base, above which there were four inches of dry earth, a six inch layer of cow hair, two inch thick timber planks, all covered by half an inch of tarred hair. A series of oval copper pipes was then laid on top, and it was these pipes which conveyed the coolant which froze the final ingredient, the water, to form the skating surface.

As for the coolant, outside the Glacarium a steam engine drove an air pump which circulated sulphuric acid, which, first condensed, then expanded by a vacuum, passed into a refrigeration unit, which... to cut a complicated process short, in the end lost the Rusholme licensee a great deal of money.

Thus the rink closed sometime in the spring of 1878, just over a year after it had opened. It was the same story in London.

But Gamgee's dream did not die yet. His fifth and largest Glacarium, on Lord Street, Southport, opened in January 1879. Costing £30,000, this one fared rather better, staying in business as Britain's only rink for the next ten years. Indeed until another opened in Frankfurt in 1881, Southport boasted the only ice rink in the world.

Rusholme's Glacarium, meanwhile lay abandoned before being replaced by the Trocadero Cinema in the early 20th century. The site is now occupied by a supermarket, its place in the early development of ice skating sadly unacknowledged.

After Southport closed in 1889, few dared to invest in ice rinks. Roller rinks, on the other hand, being cheaper to build and maintain, were more popular than ever, particularly since the introduction of maple flooring and an improved type of roller skate using ball-bearings, developed in America in 1884.

Ice rinks, meanwhile, were few and far between. Two new London rinks, opened during the 1890s, soon closed. That left one in Crossmyloof, Glasgow, opened in 1907, and the private Prince's Club in Knightsbridge, where the first Olympic skating championships were staged during the London games of 1908. But this stayed open only due to the largesse of the Duchess of Bedford.

It was at this point that all eyes in the world of ice skating turned back to Manchester.

As had been the case with John Gamgee 35 years earlier, the starting point was the obvious synergy between the developing refrigeration industry and the growing market for leisure.

In Manchester's case the new driving force was a company called Lancashire Hygienic Dairies, established in 1899 following the amalgamation of four of the city's dairies. Ice was a vital commodity for milk distributors (as it was for fishmongers, butchers, hotels, hospitals, and so on, before the advent of electrical fridges).

In 1900, therefore, after a particularly hot summer during which water had to be rationed, the dairy's directors set up a second business, the Crystal Ice Company. Various test drillings for artesian wells were carried out, before a site was chosen on the south side of Derby Street, in the back streets of Cheetham (which was also handy for the fish and meat markets in town).

But profitable though the ice business was in summer, the Crystal Ice Company had plenty of spare capacity the rest of the year.

That they considered an ice rink at all appears to have been the result of lobbying by members of both the Manchester Skating Club and the city's curling community, among them Norman Melland (who seemed to excel at every sport he tried) and his fellow all-rounder, Barlow Thistlethwaite, an international athlete and figure skater. As one of the activists would later write, 'John Frost' had hardly been 'over kind' to Manchester's skaters during the years that followed the bitterly cold winter of 1895.

To press their case the curlers enrolled the support of the manager of Glasgow's new rink, and his powers of persuasion, plus the promise of investment from other local interests, finally decided the issue.

James Kearns, founder of Lancashire Hygienic Dairies, committed his company to 'freeze, supply, provide and maintain' the proposed rink for a minimum of thirty years.

Kearns was able to fulfil this commitment by a simple expedient; the laying of a pipe under Derby Street to convey ammonia gas directly from the ice plant to the site of the new rink across the road. It could hardly have been simpler.

Not so the rink they built! Although not quite as large as the world's largest – the recently opened Berliner Eispalast, which Manchester representatives visited on a fact-finding tour – Manchester's Ice Palace was a palace indeed.

With its cavernous, vaulted main hall, its tea room and restaurant, and an almost square ice floor measuring 14,000 square feet, here was a building truly of its time; functional yet decorative, designed both for artistic and sporting excellence and for popular amusement; a true marriage of science, commerce and the arts.

EXTERIOR

The Manchester Ice Palace was opened on October 25 1910 by the skating enthusiast Lord Lytton in front of an estimated audience of 5,000 dignitaries and enthusiasts.

Everyone who was anyone in Manchester and in the skating world was in attendance, including no fewer than seven reigning world champions, each of whom displayed their skills on the ice.

Among them was the Swedish world figure-skating champion, Ulrich Salchow (after whom a favourite jumping manoeuvre is named), and the 29 year old British and Olympic Ladies champion, Florence Madeleine Syers, better known as Madge (who in 1902 »

▲ Awaiting a buyer in 2004, the **Manchester Ice Palace** is Britain's oldest surviving ice rink structure. Designed in Edwardian Baroque style by Everard Leeson, it was modelled on the world's largest indoor rink, the Berliner Eispalast, which had opened a year earlier.

The equipment needed to create the ice was housed in the Crystal Ice Company across the road, linked to the Ice Palace by a pipe carrying ammonia gas under Derby Street. That pipeline still exists today, although the rink ceased operations in 1967.

As can be seen from the inset photograph taken during the 1930s, apart from alterations to the main entrance, the exterior remains remarkably intact.

AS A BALLROOM

CAFE BALCONY

Gordon Richards displaying his prowess, 1935.

ICE PALACE, CHEETHAM, MANCHESTER.

▲ Despite its rather austere facade, the **Manchester Ice Palace** had a streamlined and dramatically articulated interior. Top lit by lunette windows and with viewing galleries at both ends, its roof's vaulted arches echoed the style of many modern concrete factories and exhibition halls of the period. Yet at the Palace these arches were fashioned not from reinforced concrete, as they might have appeared – and as would become the norm in the '20s and '30s – but from simple steel trusses boxed in by lath and plaster.

The Ice Palace was home to a number of different clubs and social activities, including ballroom dancing (*top left*) and curling (*above left*). Favoured skaters were invited by the manager, Bertram Wake, to join an exclusive Dance Club, which met for Sunday afternoon tea dances, waited upon by uniformed waitresses.

Those who were willing to arrive early in the morning and could afford the fee of 2s 6d per session, were able to enjoy half an hour of clean, clear ice, before the general public were admitted.

caused a sensation by entering a male-only competition, and winning a silver medal in the process. Women were promptly banned until a separate ladies event was set up in 1906).

Overnight the Ice Palace became one of the prime centres for skating in Europe. In 1912 it staged the World Championships and a lavish ice carnival – the first of many – at which the Duchess of Westminster presented prizes for the best costumes.

Also in 1912 the city's first ice hockey team formed (*see* p100).

Thursday night was curling night. Tuesday nights were set aside for the Manchester Skating Club, whose members espoused the older, stiffer 'English style' of figure skating, while a breakaway group calling itself the Northern Figure Skaters' Club preferred the 'International Style', which would eventually prevail.

Yet hardly had the Ice Palace established itself than it faced two crises. During the First World War it was occupied, firstly by Belgian refugees, then by a company making observation balloons. Only in late 1919 could skating resume, and that after litigation for unpaid rent and damages.

Then, as the 'Roaring Twenties' entered full swing, came an extremely tempting offer from a London syndicate hoping to cash in on the nation's latest craze, ballroom dancing, and turn the Ice Palace into a *palais de dance*.

But the skaters rallied support, and from 1919 until the opening of the Ice Club on London's Millbank in 1927, the Ice Palace was England's sole surviving rink.

During that spell it staged every national championship and, in 1924, the World Championships for the second time.

Just as importantly, when new rinks suddenly started appearing all over the country – nine in London alone between 1927 and 1935 – Manchester provided most of the professionals and instructors who staffed them. Without the Ice Palace, it was widely agreed, English competitive skating would have died out completely between the wars.

Instead, it thrived, and in the process, inevitably, the Ice Palace gradually shed some of its earlier gloss. The newer rinks were Art Deco in style, thus appealing to younger audiences. They were in locations more accessible to the public. Many were also more suited to ice hockey, one of the vogue sports of the 1930s.

Even so, unlike some of the newer rinks, the Palace stayed in business – even after it had been commandeered once again for barrage balloon making during the Second World War – and it remained as popular as ever during the late 1940s and early 1950s.

To the stars of the '20s and '30s – most notably Ethel Muckelt and Jack Page – a new generation of Manchester-trained skaters excelled at international level. Among them, two local pairs, Joan and John Slater, and Jean Westwood and Lawrence Demmy, (the latter from the neighbouring Jewish community in Cheetham Hill), dominated the world championships.

But life in the post war period was seldom easy for any ice rink operator. Even in the 1930s other income streams were continually sought, particularly during the summer off-season. By boarding over the ice the Palace management was able to stage dances. A summer cinema also ran there for many years.

But by the 1950s there were too many other rival attractions, and when a new ice rink opened on Devonshire Road, Altrincham, in 1961, it was clear to all that the Ice Palace's days were numbered.

During its final years the building went into steep decline. Eventually the ice was allowed to melt and for a short time the building struggled on as a cinema and bingo hall as part of the Mecca group. Finally closed in 1967, it would have been demolished had not Lancashire Dairies – still in business across the road – decided to convert the building into new offices and a plant for making UHT milk.

That was its role from 1985 until the dairy went into liquidation, as it were, in 2002. At the time of writing it lies empty and apparently unwanted.

Meanwhile, there are 60 rinks of various sizes and standards operating in Britain today, but since the closure of the Altrincham rink in 2003 – another major disappointment – for the first time since 1910 there is not a single rink in the city which has contributed so much to ice sports over the last hundred years and more.

WINDOW IN DINING ROOM

The Ice Palace today (*top*), and (*below*) the same window in 1936, seen from inside the dining room.

MANCHESTER LADIES' ICE HOCKEY CLUB 1931.

MANCHESTER ICE HOCKEY CLUB 1935-36
Back Row

A number of ice hockey clubs have tried and failed to establish the sport in Manchester. Above, at the Manchester Ice Palace, is the 1935 men's team, which, like most other British outfits, included Canadian imports, and the 1931 ladies' team, which did not. Still, with only rudimentary padding in those days it was no game for the meek. The oft-used expression 'the fastest game on earth' is believed to have been coined in Manchester, possibly by the journalist Terence Horsley, in the 1930s. Horsley wrote in 1936, 'You may think twice before you decide whether you are he-man enough to play this game, or even whether the risk of a cracked skull or ruined nose is worth it. But once you have seen it played, you will never hesitate to go again. Short of watching a world title fight, I know of nothing which is more thrilling.'

▼ Despite Terence Horsley's stirring commendation (left), ice hockey has never consistently managed to attract the level of crowds or investment that the game has traditionally enjoyed in the USA or Canada (where it originated in the 1860s).

Britain's first ice hockey club formed at the Prince's Club, London, in 1897. Manchester followed in 1912, becoming one of five founder members of the British Ice Hockey Association.

However, once several new London rinks joined the fray in the late 1920s and started importing Canadian players – and paying them 'expenses' – Manchester struggled. Not only was the Ice Palace the wrong shape for ice hockey, being too square, but with barely 2,000 seats it could not hope to match larger venues, such as Wembley.

Matters became so acute in the late 1930s that for one season an entire French Canadian team from Paris was brought over to Derby Street and named the **Manchester Rapids**. They bid *au revoir* after one unhappy season.

After the war, little or no competitive ice hockey was played in the Manchester area – nor indeed in many other parts of Britain – until a Northern League was formed in 1966. One of the founders then was the **Altrincham Aces**, based at the recently opened Devonshire Road rink. But again they struggled to pay their way and, in 1986, following a sponsorship deal with the local authority, they were renamed the **Trafford Metros** (*seen in action below*).

The next great leap forward for ice hockey occurred in the 1990s, but this time, interestingly, it was focused not upon ice rinks but on Britain's new generation of multi-purpose arenas, all of them designed in collaboration with American specialist architects.

The first of these to open was the Sheffield Arena, built as part of the city's hosting of the World Student Games, in 1991, and soon offering a busy programme of rock concerts, basketball, indoor tennis and, thanks to the development of artificial ice pads, ice hockey.

Similar arenas followed in Birmingham, Newcastle, Belfast and London, followed by the largest of them all – in Britain and Europe – the Nynex (now MEN) Arena at Victoria Station (*see opposite*).

At last, predicted the market analysts – seeing the popularity of Britain's first fully professional ice hockey team, the Sheffield Steelers – the British public would be freed from its strangehold diet of football, rugby and cricket, and would flock to these new, family-friendly arenas to enjoy the same sports so beloved by north Americans and other European nations.

But they were wrong.

True, in its first few seasons at the new arena, the city's newly formed ice hockey club, **Manchester Storm** did fully live up to its name by drawing the largest crowds ever known in British ice hockey. But this early promise faded all too quickly, and after attendances slumped, a replacement franchise called the **Manchester Phoenix** ended up at Altrincham before it too dropped out of the running.

The Phoenix plan to a second coming, in a new rink to be built either in Altrincham or Manchester.

But the rise and fall of both the Storm and the Phoenix suggests that, as in previous decades, ice hockey – in common with that other north American 'arena' sport, basketball – will have to work extremely hard to establish to find a lasting place in the hearts of local sports fans.

But one can be sure that ice hockey will return. It always does.

Now called the **Manchester Evening News Arena**, Europe's largest indoor arena was built as part of the city's bid for the 2000 Oympics. Costing £56m, of which £35.5m came from government grants, plus £2.5m from the European Economic Development Fund, it can accommodate up to 19,500 spectators, depending on the event.

The massive structure, half of which strides the airspace above the platforms of Victoria Station, has a lattice steel roof measuring a colossal 130 x 110m (that is *twice* the area of a football pitch). It was designed by the joint US-British partnership, DLA Ellerbe Beckett, with Ove Arup as consultant engineers and Austin-Smith:Lord as master planners.

Unlike conventional ice rinks the arena was not intended for public skating. Nevertheless, ice skating, on one of the new breed of demountable ice-pads – how John Gamgee would marvel at modern science! – provided its official opening event on July 15

1995. This was an ice spectacular by former world champions Christopher Torvill and Jayne Dean, watched by a record crowd (for an ice event) of over 15,000 people.

A further British and European record crowd for an ice hockey match, 17,425, saw **Manchester Storm** v. Sheffield Steelers on February 23 1997, while the city's other new franchise to break attendance records was the **Manchester Giants** basketball team. They drew a British record of 14,251, also in 1997, for a match against the London Leopards.

Yet like the Storm, the Giants also later folded, never to re-appear.

Both failures – and similar tales from other cities – show just how tough it is for promoters to lure British spectators away from their traditional sports.

Some would call this conservatism. Some would argue that it only proves the depth of our sporting heritage.

Whatever, in recent years the arena has rather sidestepped sport and now concentrates on concerts.

Chapter Fourteen

Lads' Clubs

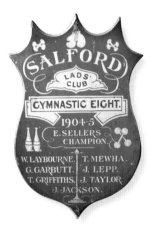

A gymnastics trophy at the Salford Lads' Club, Ordsall. Sporting activity played a critical role in attracting members. It served other purposes too. The 'dangerous classes', it was once said, would not be so dangerous if they learnt 'to play the game'.

Charles Russell, among his many roles as a social and penal reformer during the early decades of the 20th century, was the honorary secretary of the Heyrod Street Lads' Club, Ancoats.

No corner of urban Britain was rougher, tougher or more densely populated.

Nor was any part of Manchester more frequented by middle class philanthropists and moralists in search of charitable causes to fight and souls to save.

The working class boy, wrote Russell in 1905, 'is indeed a puzzling, inconsistent, and, often enough, exasperating creature. He has, it must be admitted, many disadvantages. He has little parental control, and resents restraint of any kind whatever.'

Not all was lost however. Noting that 'the rough, noisy horse-play and disorder of the artisan quarters has greatly decreased...' Russell observed that the Manchester boy 'is conscious, as soon as he becomes a wage earner, that he is contributing to the general welfare of his home... he has early learned in the over-crowded rooms of the cottage in which he lives, much that had better come to him in later years. In his early teens he knows too much of evil – and also of good, for he has seen self-denial and self-sacrifice in times of want that boys, under more fortunate circumstances, know nothing of.'

Charitable institutions for the young and vulnerable – Ragged Schools, The Manchester Mill and Working Girls Society and the like – sprang up throughout the Victorian era in the rapidly expanding industrial cities.

In 1824 the Manchester Mechanics' Institute, the first of its kind outside London, offered evening classes. Lyceums were established in the 1830s to lure young men away from the pub, complete with lounges, plush red curtains and welcoming hearths, libraries and games rooms.

But noble though their aims were, the lyceums proved too earnest for most young men after a hard day's work. Similarly, the YMCA, formed in 1844, had only limited appeal to older youths. Nor was it relevant to boys in their early teens, who may have been too young or too poor for pubs but who were just as likely to be in moral danger on the streets.

As the *Boys Own Paper* put it, by the 1870s 'there were institutions by the score to help boys who qualified by crime, but none for the honest working lad.'

Sporting activity offered one obvious safety valve. Indeed several of our leading football clubs, Manchester City included, trace their origins to attempts by church leaders to provide this kind of outlet. City began life in 1880 as the football team of St Mark's, West Gorton, following an earlier attempt by the vicar's daughter to establish a working men's club.

Back in Ancoats in 1883, one of several charitable initiatives, the Committee for Securing Open Spaces for Recreation opened, ironically, an indoor gymnasium, to encourage physical exercise.

But the first Boys' Club to be formed and specifically named as such appeared in London, in Kennington, in 1872.

It then took another 14 years for Manchester's first club to open »

The banner at the opening ceremony of the Salford Lads' Club in January 1904 sums up the founders' intentions. The Lads Club movement often veered between the robust and the sentimental, whilst expressing many of the worries still felt about boys today. Here, for example, is a verse sung at the opening of the Stockport Lads' Club in 1890:

God Bless the Boys of England, our future hope and joy,
God save them from all the Evils that threaten or destroy,
God Bless the Lads and speed them, with honour and success,
O God, who art their father, the Boys of England Bless!

An Edwardian gymnastics shield from the Salford Lads' Club. The parallel bars are still in use.

» – a few months after Liverpool's first – and when it did, it had a rather unlikely champion.

Alexander 'Lex' Devine, half Irish, half Greek, was the charismatic 21 year old editor of a weekly journal in Rusholme who discovered a capacity for leadership while teaching at Sunday School. As a reporter he also witnessed the procession of young recidivists passing through the police courts. Many belonged to street gangs, the Scuttlers and the Ikes, distinguished by their metal tipped clogs, brass-studded belts, bell-bottomed trousers and concealed razors. (In Birmingham their counterparts were called Peaky Blinders.)

Resolved both to make the streets safer and to keep teenagers out of trouble, in 1886 Devine called a meeting in Hulme to which 2,000 boys attended, many, it was said, drawn by the promise of free tea. (Charles Russell, for his part, argued that the working classes drank far too much tea.)

Suitably encouraged, Devine soon solicited support from such luminaries as Lord Aberdeen, Lord Egerton of Tatton and the *Manchester Guardian* editor CP Scott, leading to a grand opening of the Hulme and Chorlton-on-Medlock Lads' Club, in November 1886, in a disused building in Mulberry Street. (The club subsequently moved into Procter's Gymnasium, now the site of the Powerhouse, on Raby Street.)

Buoyed by this success, Devine went on to persuade the Old Boys of Manchester Grammar School – apparently against the wishes of the High Master – to sponsor the setting up of the Hugh Oldham Lads' Club (named after the school's founder) in a disused police station on Livesey Street. He then engineered a major coup by arranging for the Prince of Wales, in Manchester on other business, to open this new club. He also won support for a new Gorton and

Openshaw Lads' Club from the industrialist, Sir William Crossley.

But there, within two years, his contribution ended. According to his biographer, Devine was a supreme egotist who cared little for committees or proper accounting, and with opposition to his autocratic methods mounting, he departed Manchester for London in the company of twelve street boys and with £10 in his pocket. He would later set up a series of private schools and lecture on educational reform. His brother Henry, meanwhile, stayed on to rescue the Hulme club from the chaos left behind by Lex, while another brother entered the church and became active in London boys' club circles.

Devine would later be described by some as the Father of the Boys' Club movement, which was not true. Other made rather more personal insinuations concerning his motives. Neither he nor his brothers ever married. Yet his legacy was real enough. By 1907, 23 clubs, all created more or less on Devine's original model at Hulme, operated in the Manchester area, with a combined membership of around 10,000.

Not only was this a significantly high total – almost as many as in London – but the nature of the clubs themselves was, by all accounts, quite distinctive.

For all their emphasis on Christian education, Manchester's clubs, unlike most of their London counterparts, were non-denominational, run independently of churches or universities. Citizenship and efficiency were equally at their core. Charles Russell, who became involved around 1892 after arriving in the city to work for a railway company, urged Lads' Club workers – all unpaid volunteers – to 'look ahead; look to the man who is beyond the boy'.

Manchester clubs were, in short, not for loafers. They were for working lads. For after-work activities.

This serious intent was reflected in the solid, institutional and practical designs of the Lads' Clubs themselves. Part schools, part social clubs; part utilitarian, part homely; in addition to gymnasiums and games rooms, they featured libraries, classrooms and lounges for fire-side chats. Weekly fees had to be paid. Saving banks were encouraged. Some clubs even ran labour bureaus.

Even so, 'The compelling force which brings members to the clubs,' as Russell acknowledged, was sport and recreation.

Hence many of the clubs were superbly equipped, offering boys the only opportunity most would ever have of using proper sports equipment. However, to ensure that the physical benefits did not outweigh the moral, no member was allowed to play games until he had attended classes. A Lads' Club, Russell advised, had to be 'a benevolent despotism'.

Judged by today's standards it might be hard to discern many differences between the goings-on at a Lads' Clubs in Manchester and a Boys' Clubs in London. But in the context of Edwardian England the subtle variations in approach – the balance between play and purpose, regimentation and development, prayer and progress – seemed all important. Even Baden-Powell's scout movement was not universally admired. What use did a city boy have for camping skills?

Nevertheless various strands of the Lads' and Boys' Clubs movement did gradually merge, the result being that the National Association of Clubs for Young People is one of the largest voluntary youth organisations in Britain. Some 3,000 clubs now work with 400,000 young people, of which 40 per cent are girls.

Alexander Devine, Charles Russell and the Manchester clubs were all clearly influential in the early years of this movement.

But there is a further reason for highlighting Lads' Clubs in this study, and that is the fact that three of the oldest purpose-built club buildings surviving in Britain today are to be found in the city.

The three clubs are at Ardwick (1897), Salford (1903) and Openshaw (1912), all built during Charles Russell's time.

Relics of a byegone era they may be, but each continues to function, and as Russell himself would be the first to argue, many of the problems they were designed to address have not gone away.

▼ Opened in 1897 and designed by architects W & G Higginbottom, the Ardwick Lads' and Mens' Club (now the **Ardwick Youth Centre**), on Palmerston Street, is believed to be Britain's oldest purpose-built youth club still in use.

The Lads' Club itself was originally formed in a print works on Bridge Street, in 1889, by Paul Schill and works manager Will Melland, after whom the Melland Playing Fields on Mount Road, Levenshulme, were named. (Will was a cousin of the great all-round sportsman, Norman Melland.)

As the club grew it decamped to the nearby Mayfield Baths, where the pool was boarded up during the winter and used as a gymnasium.

The current premises, when first opened, featured a large gymnasium with viewing gallery – where the 1933 All England Amateur Gymnastics Championships were held – three fives courts, a billiard room and two skittle alleys (later converted to shooting galleries). Boxing – still a favourite – cricket, cycling, swimming and badminton were also organised, and in 1929 a boys' netball league was started.

At its peak between the two world wars, Ardwick was the Manchester area's largest club, with 2,000 members. But even today, under the ownership of Manchester City Council, it is regularly used by up to 600 people per week and, although in need of refurbishment, remains structurally sound and much loved by the local community.

▲ Tucked away discreetly from the noise and traffic of Regent Road, Ordsall, is the **Salford Lads' Club**, on the corner of St Ignatius Walk and Coronation Street (the original, no less).

A magical building, in body and spirit, it forms an integral part of the equally esteemed Barracks Estate, an early social housing scheme designed for Salford Corporation by Henry Lord, on the site of a former barracks. Along the road from the Club is the Church of St Ignatius, by Alfred Darbyshire (also 1903), and several streets of red brick terraced houses, ranged around a park square.

A Salford Working Girls' Institute – a smaller sister to the Lads' Club, as it were – stood close to the church but was destroyed during the Second World War. Also gone is the original pub on Gloucester Street (which in early episodes of

Coronation Street doubled as the Rovers Return). But even if not wholly intact, the estate remains a remarkable and historic enclave.

The Lads' Club itself, financed by the brewers JG and WG Groves and also designed by Henry Lord in 1903, is, furthermore, the finest example of a pre-First World War boys' club surviving and operating today. As an exemplar of its type it certainly ranks alongside its contemporaries, the Victoria Baths (*see p123*) and the Manchester Ice Palace (*see p97*) in national importance. It has also shared with both buildings an uncertain future. In 2001 it even faced demolition.

Since then, with the aid of club stalwarts, local campaigners, various improvements grants and an unlikely ally from the music world (*see opposite*), the club has undergone a spirited revival. Two days before its 100th anniversary

in 2003 the building was also granted Grade II listed status.

It has numerous qualities.

Lord used the irregular corner site to great advantage, respecting the scale of the estate yet creating a surprising number of large interior spaces on varying levels.

There is a full height gymnasium, a concert hall, billiard room, library (now used for IT), senior and junior gamesrooms, two classrooms, offices, entrance lodge, a kitchen and a cellar, once used for woodwork classes. The club also had three fives courts, since converted for other activities.

Many of the original details, such as the ceramic tiling, glazed partitions, beamed roofs, even the engraved labels on each door, have survived. So too has much of the original equipment and furniture, including a set of parallel bars, weights and billiard tables.

Not surprisingly, the building is in regular demand as a film set.

But the Salford Lads' Club (now officially Lads' and Girls', of course), is no museum piece. Over 200 people still visit on a weekly basis, for club gatherings, boxing and martial arts classes. It is also used for meetings, and more recently, for open days and exhibitions. A camera obscura set up under the cupola has proved particularly popular.

But the Club has recently found for itself one other role.

Thanks to the preservation of literally thousands of individual membership cards going back to 1903, plus several detailed scrap books and dozens of cine films taken at the club's annual summer camps in Wales – which still take place – the office of the Salford Lads' Club has evolved into an unofficial family archive for the whole Ordsall area.

▶ The **Salford Lads' Club** enjoys a fame which transcends its historic, social and architectural significance. In 1985, apparently drawn by the Barrack Estate's appearance in the gritty 1961 film classic, *A Taste of Honey*, and perhaps also the Coronation Street sign, a Manchester band called The Smiths decided to pose in front of the Lads' Club's front door.

When the image later appeared on their album *The Queen is Dead* officials of the club were not best pleased. In fact they threatened legal action against the photographer, Stephen Wright. Yet this single image would, in time, attract so many pilgrims from around the world that the club has set aside a whole room devoted to the band. (Wright's photo, meanwhile, now hangs in the Manchester Art Gallery.)

Lord Baden-Powell, the founder of the scout movement who was guest of honour at the club's official opening in 1904 (*see p103*), would no doubt have been horrified by the miserablist philosophy of The Smiths' leading sage, Morrissey. Then, as now, the club's motto was 'to brighten young lives and make good citizens'. Even when playing billiards or cards *(below)* members were expected to refrain from swearing, gambling and bad sportsmanship.

But if the regime sounds strict, the club was actually for many years one of Salford's favourite social centres.

Boxers Henry Cooper and Terry Downs, and actor Albert Finney, would often stop by, as would Bobby Charlton and other Busby Babes after United home games. On the night of the 1958 Munich disaster – in which former member Eddie Colman died – the club opened its doors to mourning supporters.

Other former members were Tony Holland (the Muscle Man on TV's *Opportunity Knocks*), artist Harold Riley, and both Graham Nash and Allan Clarke of The Hollies, who rehearsed there.

Sport and the arts have thus always been at the heart of the club's existence. As Morrissey wrote, and as friends of Salford Lads' Club continue to insist, 'There is a light that never goes out.'

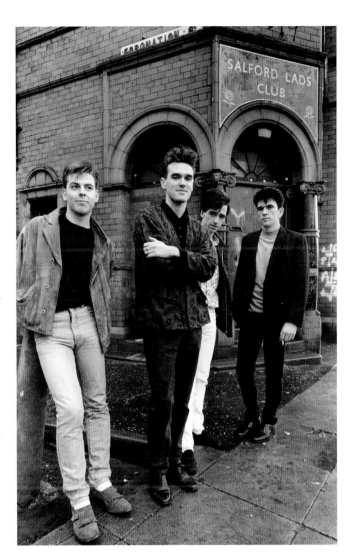

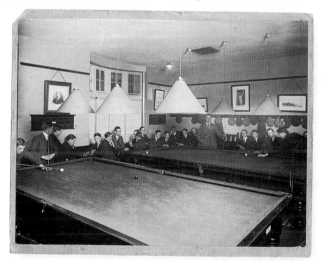

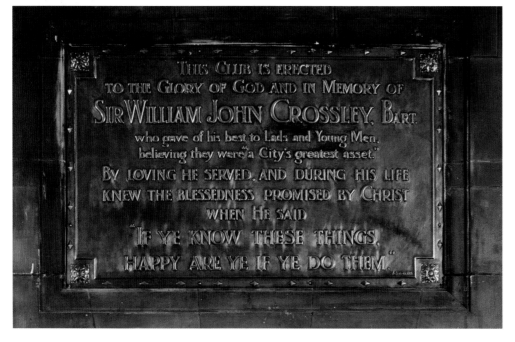

◄ **Crossley House Youth Centre** on Ashton Old Road was originally home to the Gorton and Openshaw Working Lads' Club. It was designed by John Broadbent of Altrincham and opened in 1913, although the datestone states 1912. (For its first few months the building served as a hospital during an outbreak of consumption.)

The Lads' Club, the third of its kind to be established in the city, formed originally in 1888 after Alexander Devine enrolled the support of Sir William Crossley, a teetoal Liberal MP, whose substantial engineering works were then close by in Pottery Lane. (Crossley's brother, Frank, went one further in philanthropic endeavour by living and working amongst the poor, in Ancoats, naturally.)

Sir William was one of the first Lads' Club sponsors to stipulate that boys attending camps should regularly attend a place of worship and evening school. 'Lads and young men,' he believed, 'were a city's greatest asset,' and four members of Openshaw proved him right by going on to become Lord Mayors of Manchester.

As is true of Ardwick Lads' Club, Crossley House is no architectural gem. Nor is it wholly suited to the needs of today's youth. Problems with access, maintenance and security cannot be masked indefinitely. Its surroundings have

also changed beyond recognition as the result of slum clearance, factory closures and urban redevelopment.

However, the building remains in active use for up to 700 people a week, and retains at least some elements of its original character.

An open-plan lounge with a manorial-style fireplace – above which a copper memorial plaque to Sir William still hangs (*left*) – is a reminder that for many boys from deprived homes the club was a place to seek warmth as well as friendship, as they sat around the hearth to hear stories or engage in organised discussion. Adjacent to this is a spacious billiard room.

The building also has a 500 seat assembly hall, no longer fit for use, with an elevated rear gallery where Lady Crossley would sit in throne-like isolation. Each boy was expected to bow to her on entering the hall. At the rear, a 'rough house' area used for indoor football, handball and other games (*above*) has its own gallery, still with its original parquet floor, cambered to form a running track.

Next door to Crossley House is the former **Whitworth Baths**, funded – as was the Whitworth Art Gallery – by that other prominent engineer and philanthropist of Victorian Manchester, Sir Joseph Whitworth, in 1890, but now boarded up (see p120).

Seemingly stranded, Crossley House and the Whitworth Baths form a poignant pair, as the 21st century through traffic rushes past.

▲ The **Stockport Lads' Club**, set in five acres of playing fields on Hempshaw Lane, is a rare example of a post-war Lads' Club. Opened in 1960, it replaced the club's original building, designed by Darbyshire and Smith in 1889 and still extant on Wellington Street, albeit boarded-up, having been used in recent years as a glove factory.

Stockport was one of the busiest lads' clubs of the 1890s, with a reported 7,000 members, most of whom were described as having homes 'not sufficiently attractive to draw them from street corners'.

Today, 40 clubs are affiliated to the Greater Manchester Federation of Clubs for Young People, all run entirely by volunteers. Stockport's Harry Wright MBE, has been active in the club since 1945, and there are others like him all over Britain.

The region's oldest club, on Cannon Street, Salford, is the **Adelphi Lads' Club**, founded in 1888. Its modest headquarters date back to 1910. However the newest and best equipped premises belong to the **Bolton Lads' and Girls' Club**, Spa Road, Bolton, designed by Michael Hyde and Associates and opened in 2002 thanks to a £4 million Sport England Lottery grant – the largest ever awarded to a voluntary club – plus a further £1 million raised locally. The club has already won awards, as has one of its members, the teenage boxer, Amir Khan, who famously won a silver medal at the 2004 Athens Olympics.

Chapter Fifteen

Billiards

For over two centuries publicans traded on the popularity of billiards, and its late Victorian offshoot, snooker. But in recent years smaller and more profitable American pool tables have gained in popularity, so that relatively intact billiard rooms such as the one at The Lamb Hotel, Regent Street, Eccles (1906) are increasingly rare.

Mary Queen of Scots loved billiards, as did Louis XIV. But in 1757 the Whig government decided that the game encouraged gambling, and threatened £10 fines for any publicans caught with tables on their premises. Clearly this failed. By 1801, Joseph Strutt, author of encyclopaedic *Sports and Pastimes of the People of England,* felt billiards to be 'so generally known' that no further description was deemed necessary.

In Manchester as elsewhere, billiards and, since the late 1920s, its sister game snooker, has mostly been played in purpose-built basements (such as that of the Grosvenor Palace Cinema, Oxford Road, built 1915), or in halls above or behind shops or cafés. As such its presence in our midst has remained largely anonymous.

This invisibility rather accords with the game's traditional image. A billiards or snooker hall is where young men supposedly hide away during their 'mis-spent youth'. 'Billiard sharks,' lamented one Edwardian moralist, found the game's wiles 'more seductive than the call of home or friends'.

But that is no reason to exclude billiards from the wider canon of our sporting heritage.

On the contrary, over the centuries the game's aesthetic has inspired some of Britain's leading designers – Edwin Lutyens and Charles Rennie Mackintosh included – to create a number of delightful and original billiard rooms for the country house set and for a range of commercial clients, while billiard tables and accessories are to be found in all manner of styles; Edwardian Baroque, Art Nouveau, and Arts and Crafts among them.

Moreover, in the richly-detailed buildings commissioned by the Temperance Billiard Halls company, founded in Rusholme in 1906 (*see* p112), Manchester once possessed some of the finest examples of purpose built halls known in Edwardian England.

The exact origins of billiards are unclear. Most often credited are the French, who, in around the 16th century, transferred a game similar to croquet from outdoors to indoors, and from ground level to a cloth-covered table top.

What is certain is that the modern table and its fixtures and fittings were developed by John Thurston, a former apprentice at the Gillow furniture factory in London, who set up on his own in 1799. (The Thurston name still trades today, from Liverpool.)

In 1826 Thurston pioneered the all important insertion of slate beds under the table's surface, to improve the run of the balls. In 1835 he introduced rubber cushions, which he further improved in 1849 by using newly invented vulcanised rubber.

As Thurston's designs gradually evolved, the familiar six-pocket table measuring 12 x 6 feet that we use today was finally adopted as the standard in 1892.

By the 1930s billiard halls were everywhere. Manchester had nearly 40, and that was in addition to the tables found in virtually every sports club, working men's club, lads' club and gentleman's club. Hotels and pubs found room too, building extensions if necessary. Like juke-boxes or mini-gyms in later years, billiard tables were all the rage, with an army »

▲ **The Lamb Hotel**, Regent Street, Eccles – designed for the Holt's brewery by a Mr Newton of Hartley, Hacking & Co. – retains several typically Edwardian interior details, not least in its rich wood panelling and well preserved billiards room.

Note how the raised banquettes, which sit above cast iron radiators, allow drinkers to observe the action in comfort, as if the room were an indoor stadium, with the green baize as the pitch.

Billiard tables are exceptionally durable. This one, made by the London firm of Burroughes & Watts, is the original, supplied when the Lamb first opened in 1906. As can be seen in the near corner, its leather trimmed pockets hang over open sided rails for potted balls to slide down; a style patented in 1899 by the Burnley firm of Willie

Holt (no relation to the brewers), and one which superceded closed pockets, from which it was harder to extract the balls, once potted.

The scoreboard (*right*), also from 1906, was supplied by Raper and Sons, of Stevenson Square, one of seven billiard and bagatelle manufacturers based in Manchester at the time. On either side of the blackboard are sliding wooden slats (now fixed). These were used to score a once popular game called life pool, in which up to 13 players competed – imagine the scene! – each with their own coloured ball and three lives to play for.

Also in Eccles is the Grapes Hotel, Liverpool Road (1903). Both this and the Lamb are listed Grade II and are on the Campaign for Real Ale's national inventory of historic pub interiors. But at the

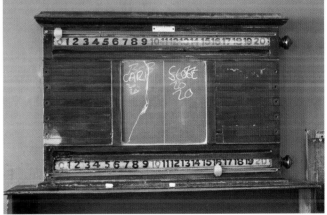

Grapes a pool table now occupies the billiards room. If only life pool had stayed in fashion, perhaps the original table might have paid its way. Time for another CAMRA campaign, perchance?

▶ The **Sedge Lynn** pub on Manchester Road, Chorlton, is a head-turning delight, rescued from near dereliction by the Weatherspoons chain in 1998 and now listed Grade II.

Before becoming a pub, for many years the building was well known in Manchester as the Chorlton Snooker Club, once the regular haunt of the wayward snooker genius, Alex Higgins.

What is less well known is that the building was originally – and ironically, considering its current use – a temperance billiard hall.

Designed by the in house architect of the Temperance Billiard Halls Company, Norman Evans, the building opened in 1907, and is now the finest surviving example of the dozen or so playful and decorative halls he designed between 1906-10.

As if to compensate for the absence of alcohol on sale, each Evans hall was a visual treat; an eclectic mix of cupolas, oriel windows, overhanging eaves and brightly painted keystones, set against white, roughcast walls. This was cheap and cheerful leisure architecture; a touch of California in the Manchester suburbs.

The interior at Chorlton (*right*), though much altered, retains its original dormer windows and Art Nouveau glazing. Above all, quite literally, is its wonderfully simple barrel-vaulted roof, supported by basic timber trusses, bolted together using steel plates, each stamped in an Arts and Crafts style.

Contrary to most dimly lit billiard halls, Evans flooded his interiors with natural light in an attempt to attract middle class custom.

Less well preserved is his 1906 hall in Cheetham Hill Road (*far right*), also Grade II, now used as a fruit and vegetable warehouse.

of competing sales representatives pressing their wares.

Simply to meet the demand for balls, it has been estimated, some 12,000 elephants were slaughtered in just one year during the 1890s. (Composite substitutes would not be perfected until the 1920s.) Apparently it took one tusk to fashion five balls.

Dozens of manufacturers emerged, seven in Manchester alone by 1927, and in order to control the market further, some started to operate their own halls.

Thurston's, in Leicester Square, London, remained the most prestigious until it was bombed in 1940. (It was apparently a favourite haunt of JB Priestley.)

But in the north the name of EJ Riley held sway. Edward Riley was an Accrington man who, in 1878, gave up banking to open a sports shop. He then started manufacturing, first cricket bats, then billiard tables. So successful was he that by 1900 EJ Riley Ltd was challenging the established London firms, such as Thurston's and Burroughes & Watts.

Riley's greatest coup came when two top players – probably swayed by an under-the-table envelope – chose a Riley table for the 1903 professional championships, much to the ire of the Billiards Association members who were linked to Riley's rivals. By 1910 the company was selling 4,000 tables a year. (They were manufactured at Willow Mills, Accrington, which famously had a 120 yard long workshop used for training by the sprinter Max Whittenburgh.)

Riley's largest billiard outlet was Ardwick Hall, opened in 1910 with 40 tables. But there would be dozens more opened and acquired over the next 70 years, many of which still operate

under the Riley name (although the manufacturing arm of the company collapsed in 2001).

Riley halls were not designed in a particular style, often being set up in converted buildings. In contrast, the Temperance Billiard Halls Company of Rusholme created a distinctive brand that would be instantly recognisable.

Norman Evans was the company architect, appointed in 1906 after serving his articles at Brameld and Smith. In three years, Evans designed possibly as many as 20 halls in the Manchester area, the flagship outlet being on Wilmslow Road, Rusholme, in what is now an Indian restaurant. Other surviving halls converted to various uses are in Hyde Road, Stretford Road and, shown opposite, Cheetham Hill and Chorlton.

Yet although by 1939 the tables were as popular as ever, the game being played was no longer billiards. In just a few short years snooker had swept the nation. Simpler to play and better to watch than billiards, the game was invented by British officers serving in Jubblepore, India, in 1875. A *snooker*, in army slang, was a rookie at Woolwich's Military Academy.

But if billiards fell moribund, as the snooker world was to discover in the 1950s and 1960s, the trouble with being fashionable is that fashions soon change. And change again. Colour television would transform snooker's appeal from 1969 onwards, making it more popular than ever. But in the 1990s the game of pool started racking up the points.

Played on smaller tables which offer higher yields to pubs and hall operators, could this American import be yet one more threat to the sporting heritage of Britain?

▲ Shown here in 1940, the Openshaw branch of **Burton's**, on the corner of Ashton Old Road and Grey Mare Lane (now Alan Turing Way), was one of 600 distinctive stores built by the 'The Tailor of Taste' and was typical of the work of the company architect from 1928-38, N Martin.

The company's founder, Montague Burton, a Jewish refugee who in 1900 started work as a pedlar in Chesterfield, was keen that his stores should not intimidate working-class men.

The buildings had therefore to appeal to masculine tastes; to be modern, yet restrained, and preferably be located on a corner site, for maximum impact. In order to keep customers happy while they waited for their suits to be

adjusted – and also to encourage more men to pass by – Burton rented out the upper floors of many of his shops as billiard halls.

At a time when thousands of men were inspired to take up the cue by the much publicised matches of the Davis brothers, Joe and Fred – snooker's first superstars – it was a winning ploy.

Former Burton's stores are easy to identify. Some, as at 122 Oldham Street (which had two floors of tables) retain their foundation stones, inscribed always in a black polished stone described once as 'Montague Burtonite'. It is also possible to find former Burton's with snooker clubs still operating, as in Eccles, for example, where the upper floor doubled as a dance hall during the 1950s.

Chapter Sixteen

Air Racing

LOUIS PAULHAN (1883-1963)
PIONEER FRENCH AVIATOR LANDED
A FARMAN BILANE IN A FIELD ON
THIS SITE MAKING THE FIRST
LONDON/MANCHESTER FLIGHT
28TH APRIL 1910

Odd though it may seem to consider air racing as a sport, there was a time when huge crowds gathered to watch pilots compete in trials of speed and endurance, just as they do for today's Grand Prix motor racing. Daring and dangerous, flying was a modern marvel that had to be seen to be believed.

The north west was at the forefront of early aviation. Britain's first authorised aviation meeting took place in Blackpool in October 1909. A Manchester Aero Club then formed and in March 1910 organised an aircraft exhibition at White City, Old Trafford.

A month later Manchester welcomed its first celebrity aviator, Louis Paulhan, a Frenchman who challenged an English rival, Claude Grahame-White, for the *Daily Mail's* prize of £10,000 for the first pilot to fly from London to Manchester. The distance had to be covered in 24 hours, with only two stops allowed en route. When the challenge was first issued in 1906 the furthest any European had flown was 220 yards.

Paulhan took off from Hendon on April 27, watched by 4,000 onlookers. Another 15,000 were at Wormwood Scrubs to see Grahame-White frustrated by high winds. Well in the lead, Paulhan overnighted at Lichfield, then spent the early hours of April 28 following railway lines from Crewe, before landing at 5.32am in a field in Burnage, where thousands of Mancunians, businessmen and factory workers alike, had gathered. As *The Times* reported, no one cared that it was the Frenchman who triumphed. 'It was enough that he was a hero of the air.'

By the time the next *Daily Mail* air race hit town – this time a 1,000 mile Round Britain challenge, also worth £10,000 – Manchester had its first designated airfield.

This was a grass strip, laid out on Trafford Park's former deer park, on Ashburton Road, opposite the recently built Westinghouse works. Lt Conneau of the French Navy won the race.

But the French were not the only high-fliers. By 1912 the Mancunian AV Roe (born in Patricroft in 1877), had returned to the city to set up his first aircraft manufacturing company, on Great Ancoats Street. Roe tested one of the first Avro designs at Eccles Cricket Ground in June 1912.

After 1918 flying activities in the city switched from Trafford Park to a new airfield called Alexandra Park (named after a railway station, no longer in use, south of the current park of that name).

Alexandra Park accepted Manchester's first ever civil flight, from Oxford, in May 1919. It was also where, a month later, crowds welcomed back Alcock and Brown, who had first met in the city, after their epic crossing of the Atlantic.

The Lancashire Aero Club also formed at Alexandra Park, in 1922.

Had Manchester Corporation been successful in persuading

Louis Paulhan's early morning arrival in Burnage in April 1910 was greeted by a large and excited crowd, some of whom had marked the landing field with white towels. A plaque (*above*) in Paulhan Road, marks his landing site.

Lord Egerton of Tatton to sell the land, Alexandra Park would have become Britain's first municipal airport. Instead, it remained undeveloped and, in 1945, was laid out as we know it today, as the Hough End playing fields.

The Corporation, meanwhile, found an alternative site across the border in Salford, at Barton.

Inhabitants of this former village were already quite used to seeing new modes of transport arrive on their doorstep. First there was the Bridgewater Canal, often billed as Britain's first canal, opened in 1763, followed in 1830 by the world's first passenger railway line, traversing the notorious bog of Chat Moss, just north of Barton, on its way from Manchester to Liverpool.

Parallel to the railway line, the Manchester Ship Canal – the 'Big Ditch' – was next, slicing Barton in half in 1894. And now came Britain's first municipal airport, opened in 1930 and serving Manchester for the next eight years until the larger, less boggy site at Ringway finally took over in 1938.

In the context of sport, Barton was for many years a favourite port of entry for riders and owners competing at Castle Irwell racecourse. It also hosted numerous air races, including a leg of the King's Cup on July 5 1930, which drew an astonishing crowd of 30,000 to the aerodrome and its surrounding fields. Even better, the race was won by a local butcher's daughter, Winifred Brown, an intrepid member of the Lancashire Aero Club and an English hockey international to boot. (Two years later at the Manx Air Races Brown flew so low over the crowd that her Avro Avian's wheels clipped a woman watching from the top of a hedge. Air races were not for the faint-hearted.)

Peter Eckersley, captain of the Lancashire CCC, was another LAC member. In 1935 he arranged for Lancashire to become the first county cricket team to travel to a match by air. Five years later he was killed in a flying accident.

Nowadays recreational flying is for pleasure rather than for competition, and the LAC is more

popular than ever, with over 700 members. This makes it one of the largest of Britain's 70 or more aero clubs, as well as being the oldest still in operation.

But in 2002 this unique corner of aviation history suddenly seemed at risk when Manchester City Council sold the aerodrome to the property company Peel Holdings, thus raising understandable fears that the site – close to the Trafford Centre (also owned by Peel) and both the M60 and M62 motorways – would be redeveloped. These fears were eased by the subsequent listing of two other buildings on the site; the aerodrome's original hangar (which, ironically still bears the City of Manchester crest on its rear wall), and the original passenger terminal, both dating from 1930.

Should it survive, Barton could well find itself part of a new cluster of sports venues, for Peel is involved in plans for a new stadium for the Salford Reds (*see* p61) across the road from the aerodrome, and a new racecourse for Manchester in nearby Worsley.

From 1918-29, the site we now know as the Hough End playing fields (*above left*) was known as the Alexandra Park airfield.
The aerodrome at Barton, which replaced it as Manchester's main airport in 1930, has three listed buildings, including the 1933 control tower (*above*), said to be the world's oldest still in use, and surely one of the most handsome. Designed specifically to house the latest radio equipment available by the City of Manchester's Architects Department under G Noel Hill, the octagonal tower sits on a podium featuring four radiating wings, each aligned to a point of the compass.

Chapter Seventeen

Swimming

The South Manchester Swimming Club's programme for their tour of Cheltenham, Bristol and Weston-Super-Mare in 1949. The club, formed in 1930 by a merger between the Victoria Ladies and the Longsight Gents Club, was based at the Victoria Baths. Entry to one of the club's water polo matches cost 1d (0.5p).

There is no such thing as an innocent splash when it comes to the provision of public swimming pools. This is a fraught business; the subject of parliamentary select committees, government reports and, not least, frequent wrangles in town halls.

More lottery funds – £281 million as of mid 2004 – have been spent on facilities for swimming than on any other sport. Yet it is never enough. Swimming pools swallow money, raise hackles and are rarely closed without a fight.

Swimming is Britain's most popular physical recreation after walking. A public pool is considered a necessity rather than a luxury. Rather as public libraries do far more than issue books, so pools offer much more than a place to swim. For all ages, for all levels of ability, they offer training, therapy, and above all, a sensory escape from the strains and vibrations of the outside world.

Yet to refurbish all of Britain's existing pools, it has been estimated by the government, would cost between £2-3 billion. Keeping politics, finance and high emotion out of the pool is therefore well nigh impossible.

Then there is the issue of historic value.

A number of public baths may be considered amongst this country's finest examples of 19th and 20th century civic architecture. Of some 80 listed examples, seven are ranked Grade II*, of which two are in Manchester: Greengate Baths, Collier Street, Salford, dating from 1856 – regarded as this country's first modern baths – and the Victoria Baths, Hathersage Road – swimming's Taj Mahal – opened in 1906.

A further three Grade II listed baths are the Blackfriars Street Baths, Salford (1880), Harpurhey Baths, Rochdale Road (1910), and, just outside the city, Henry Square Baths, Ashton-under-Lyne (1870).

All five buildings share one characteristic. They are no longer used for swimming.

Of most concern, Greengate Baths – Britain's second oldest surviving municipal baths building (after Liverpool's Cornwallis Street baths, built 1851) – has remained on English Heritage's *Buildings at*

Risk Register since 1998, after many years serving as a warehouse.

But it is not only boarded-up Victorian baths that are under threat. In recent years the outstanding Urmston Baths, built in 1933, was closed in 1987; Sharston Baths, opened 1961, was closed in 1989, and, even more controversially, the Gorton Tub, on Garratt Way, closed in 2001 after a mere 12 years in service.

This pattern is hardly new. Britain's first municipal baths, at St George's Pier Head, Liverpool in 1829, was also shortlived.

But, it was at least a start.

The public funding of baths as we know it today began in 1846 with the Baths and Wash-houses Act. This gave local authorities the power to borrow public money to erect public washing and laundry facilities, on condition that the rates would have to cover any running losses, and that admission charges were pegged at no higher than four pence.

Given the risks entailed, only eight authorities took advantage of the Act in its early years, Liverpool and Preston included. »

Now derelict, the 1856 Greengate Baths by Thomas Worthington (*opposite*), on the corner of Collier Street and Rolla Street, is the second oldest public baths extant in Britain. Regarded as the prototype for all subsequent baths, it offered 1st and 2nd class pools for men, while women had their own entrance for the laundry and slipper baths (*far right*). Living quarters for the baths manager were provided in the attic storey. The influence of Worthington's 1848 Italian tour can be discerned in the façade and the 60 feet high, campanile-style chimney (demolished), a feature much copied by subsequent architects. As a prototype, the baths suffered from various faults and closed after less than 25 years use.

Aug. 14, 1858.] THE BUILDER. 555

MAYFIELD BATHS AND LAUNDRIES, MANCHESTER.—Mr. Thomas Worthington, Architect.

In Manchester, despite urgings from the *Manchester Guardian* for the creation of public baths following 33 drownings in the city during 1843, it was philanthropists and private companies who took the lead.

A fancy dress ball in the Free Trade Hall helped raised £440 towards the conversion of a house in Miller Street in 1846, 'to provide the poorer classes with the means of bathing themselves in tepid water'. This was followed in 1850 by the opening of a second baths, part funded by a £2,000 donation from the philanthropic banker, Sir Benjamin Heywood, on Sycamore Street, Miles Platting. Modelled on Liverpool's Paul Street baths, it featured a plunge pool measuring 27 x 16 feet, to promote exercise.

Suitably impressed by the small profits generated by these two early baths, in 1854 Manchester's aldermen decided to dip their toes into the water, as it were, by supporting the launch of the Manchester and Salford Baths and Laundries Company, with 7,000 shares issued at £5 each.

Greengate Baths, completed two years later, was the company's first construction.

A groundbreaking one it was too. Its design was by Thomas Worthington (1826-1909), a gifted young architect who had recently set up office in King Street and who went on to design *inter alia* Manchester's Albert Memorial, the Crown Court (Minshull Street) and a number of Unitarian churches, hospitals and public institutions.

A few years earlier, when he was barely 23 and only just returned from a tour of Europe (undertaken, of all times, during 1848, a year of revolutions across the continent), Worthington had entered the competition to design the halls for the 1851 Great Exhibition. Although not successful, his submission caught the eye and he was appointed to design a new glass-house for the Botanical Gardens at Old Trafford (*see* p23). This opened in 1854 but was dismissed by critics as too elaborate. Still, the experience would stand him in good stead for the baths he was about to design for the Manchester and Salford Baths and Laundries Company.

Indeed Greengate Baths established a model that would serve future designers remarkably well over the next half century.

It had two pools, first and second class, each 53 x 25 feet, with depths ranging from 3-6 foot.

Both glazed roofs were supported by weight-saving and cost-saving trusses constructed from an early form of laminated timber, rising from cantileverd iron brackets which were themselves cross braced by »

The Mayfield Baths, New Store Street, Ardwick (1856-57) was Thomas Worthington's second attempt at this still experimental building type. As at Greengate Baths he used an early form of laminated timber for the roof members, with cast iron columns doubling as drainpipes, demonstrating once more how adeptly Victorian architects married traditional architectural styles with innovative methods. Because of complaints about condensation at Greengate Baths, Worthington introduced four large vents in the roof. The building, located on the southern bank of the Medlock, approximately where Nether Street is now, was damaged by bombs in 1941, and was later demolished.

The magnificent baths in **Henry Square**, Ashton-under-Lyne, by Henry Paull and George Robinson – specialists otherwise in church architecture – was the largest of its kind in Britain when opened in 1870, thanks to a £16,000 donation by the enlightened mill owner and local MP Hugh Mason (who also endowed a library, gymnasium and recreation ground).

Known locally as Hugh Mason House, its Italian Renaissance inspired chimney is a fine example of how, following in the wake of Thomas Worthington at Salford, Victorian and Edwardian baths architects each added their own, instantly identifiable flourish.

As was the norm at the time, Ashton's main pool, 100 x 40 feet *(below left, shown in its disused state)* was reserved for men, apart from one three-hour session on Thursday afternoons. The women's pool, meanwhile, measured a rather more modest 25 x 18 feet.

Other parts of the building housed bathrooms, a Turkish bath, a police station and a fire engine.

As was also common, in winter the main pool was boarded over for use as a roller skating rink and for concerts, for which up to 4,000 people could attend.

Since closing in 1977 the building's future has been the subject of much speculation, but it is now hoped to retain the structure as part of a wider redevelopment of the immediate surrounds.

▲ Finding practical and affordable uses for former swimming baths is one of the toughest challenges facing conservationists in urban Britain today. But for the Grade II listed **Harpurhey Baths**, Rochdale Road, that challenge has been met.

Closed in 2001, the baths' laundry and its women's pool have been demolished. But the chimney has been retained, as has the entrance block and main pool (*top*), and these will form part of a new Sixth Form College for the Manchester College of Arts and Technology, combined with a new public library. The pool itself is to be converted into an art gallery. A new Harpurhey pool is meanwhile set to open nearby in early 2005. Not so fortunate is the now derelict **Whitworth Baths** (*above*), next door to Crossley House on Ashton Old Road. Designed in 1890 by JW Beaumont, this was the last privately-financed public baths built in Manchester, courtesy of Joseph Whitworth, the engineering magnate.

》 timber. The iron columns supporting the galleries doubled as drainpipes for the first floor bathrooms, where individual baths, called slipper baths, were set out for hire.

Considering the apparent grandeur of its Italianate arcaded façade, Greengate Baths was surprisingly economical to build, at just under £10,000. But such was its popularity – 18,500 users in its first year (including, it is said, the legendary Salford swimmer and saver of many lives on the River Irwell, Mark Addy) – that the Baths and Laundry Company handed Worthington a larger budget for his second commission.

This was the Mayfield Baths, New Store Street, Ardwick, built in 1856-7 at a cost of £24,660. As illustrated in *The Builder* (*see* p118), Worthington created a Paxton-like interior of immense light and depth, with two pools larger than Greengate Baths and an even taller Italianate chimney, 100 feet tall.

Worthington's third effort, similar to Greengate Baths in design and cost, was on Leaf Street, Hulme, built in 1858-60 (demolished 1976), shortly after his second tour of Italy. This had the longest pool so far, at 75 feet (just under 23m), a measure that would remain standard for some years (compared with the 25m norm today). Leaf Street also had the city's first publicly-operated Turkish Bath. (A private Turkish Bath, opened a year earlier at the Poplars, Broughton Lane, was actually the first ever in Britain.)

The company also opened a smaller Penny Bath, near Mayfield, built specifically for boys. This however was soon converted into a bath-house, following complaints about boys begging outside for money to use the facility.

By the mid 1870s the baths and laundry company's three main pools were attracting 50,000 users a year. This clear success, combined with moves in parliament to widen the scope of the 1846 Act, finally persuaded Manchester Corporation to take over the company's assets in 1879 and start a new programme of construction in those parts of the city yet to benefit.

One of the first decisions of the newly formed Baths and Wash-houses Committee was to launch a competition for the design of public baths 'in plain style of architecture and free from any elaborate ornament'. John Johnson, a London architect responsible for several town halls of the period, was chosen.

Johnson's first design for the Corporation was the New Islington Baths on Baker Street, Ancoats, opened in 1880, followed by Osborne Street Baths, Miles Platting (1883). There was then a gap before JH Maybury designed Gorton Baths on Hyde Road for the Corporation, in 1890.

Salford Corporation, meanwhile, which inherited only one baths from the former company – Greengate Baths – embarked upon its own building programme.

Greengate had not been a lasting success (as has been the fate of many a prototype pool since). But it was popular, and in an area of genuine social need. Salford's first public baths, designed by the borough engineers Brockbank and Wormall, was therefore built nearby on Blackfriars Street, in 1880. The building was completed at the same time as the adjacent Manchester Tennis and Racquet Club (*see* p87).

Ironically it was Greengate's conversion into a warehouse in the 1880s which saved it from instant demolition. Indeed both Greengate and Blackfriars Street Baths (also later converted into a warehouse) are the only Victorian baths surviving in Salford; proof, if ever it were needed, of the importance of finding alternative uses for decommissioned historic pools.

Other Salford baths built at Pendleton (1885), Great Clowes Street (1891), and Regent Road (1892), have all been demolished.

It was during this period that competitive swimming emerged as a spectator sport in Manchester.

In 1889, for example, the world's first recognised swimming record was recorded at the New Islington Baths, by a Leeds swimmer, ET 'Stivie' Jones, for the 200 yards freestyle. Meanwhile, queues built up every Tuesday and Thursday nights to see the city's newest sporting heroes, the Osborne Street water polo team.

Water polo had first evolved in the 1870s as a novelty event to entertain spectators in between races at swimming galas. Its early years were dominated by the Osborne Street team who, under the guidance of baths superintendent, John Derbyshire, won the national water polo title every year from 1894-1900. When Britain won gold medals at the Olympics of 1900, 1908, 1912 and 1920, it was swimmers from the Manchester area, including the much admired George Wilkinson from Hyde, who stole the show.

No doubt buoyed by the public's enthusiasm for all things aquatic, but more importantly, resolved also to spend the city's burgeoning wealth from industry and the Ship Canal on prestigious social welfare projects, Manchester Corporation launched its most ambitious construction programme yet. Between 1903-13 baths were opened at Moss Side (1906), Bradford (1909), Harpurhey (1910) and Withington (1913).

But most opulent of all was the Victoria Baths, in Chorlton-upon-Medlock.

Built between 1903-06, the Victoria Baths set a standard scarcely matched before or since. It was also intended as a showpiece for the city's swimming elite, being the first in the city to specifically feature a 'gala pool' with a large seated gallery for spectators. (Earlier pools had galleries, but not on this scale.)

Visiting the area today one has to ask, why did the Corporation choose here?

Firstly, they were seeking somewhere to serve Longsight, St Luke's and Rusholme, three heavily populated wards that at as yet had no modern baths. The site they eventually chose – belonging to the Victoria Park Tennis Club – sat on the border of all three.

Secondly, owing to its proximity to the university, the new hospitals around Oxford Road, and to the gated enclave of Victoria Park, the new baths could also draw on a comparatively middle-class catchment area.

Thirdly, Hathersage Road was at this time called High Street, and was a much busier thoroughfare than now.

Planning for the Victoria Baths began in 1897 in the City Surveyor's office of T de Courcy Meade. These plans, in which George Meek, architect of the Free Library on Deansgate (1882) might also have had a hand, were then taken on in 1902 by the newly appointed City Architect, Henry

Price. Over the next four testing years, it would be Price who pushed for higher standards and the use of modern technology, whilst often having to defend the project's spiralling costs.

But however lavish its decor – shown in more detail on the following pages – it should not be forgotten that for many users of the Victoria Baths, and its counterparts, the buildings had a largely practical, as well as a recreational purpose.

In 1928 one quarter of all people attending public baths in Manchester went there to wash. Even by 1951, 48 per cent of all households in Salford and 31 per cent in Manchester were still without their own bathroom.

Until they were closed in the early 1980s, the laundries also formed a vital part of the daily working lives of thousands of women unable to afford their own domestic appliances.

Manchester's early swimming baths were different from today's for other, quite practical reasons. »

▲ Although not referred to as lidos, as was the fashion elsewhere during the 1920s and 1930s, a number of open air pools were built in Manchester's public parks, including this one, thought to be at **Alexandra Park**, opened in 1934. (The photograph is from a municipal parks manual written by the former chairman of Manchester's Parks Committee, William Pettigrew, see p133).

Manchester's first open air pool predated the lido era, however.

This was laid out in 1892 at **Philips Park**, on a site north of Fairclough Street, and measured a generous 200 x 70 feet (compared with 150 x 63 feet for later installations). In 1912 the pool was used by members of the predominantly Mancunian British water polo team to acclimatise themselves to the outdoor conditions they were set to face at the Stockholm Olympics of that year. Clearly the regime worked because they won the gold.

Perhaps owing to maintenance costs, or because their popularity declined after the Second World War following a series of cooler summers, none of the city's open air pools lasted beyond the 1950s. Philips Park was, for example, decommissioned in 1949.

Opened 1913, Withington is Manchester's oldest baths still in use. Designed by the City Architect's department under Henry Price, it underwent a £1m revamp in 2004. Price's successor, G Noel Hill, adopted a plainer neo-Georgian style for the city's inter-war designs, of which Broadway Baths, New Moston, 1932 (below), was the last.

» Until water filtration units – first installed at the Victoria Baths – became standard, Manchester's swimming pools were essentially water-filled tanks.

On the first day of the weekly cycle they were filled with fresh clean water. For this day the admission price was at its highest. Then, as the days went by, inevitably the water grew steadily murkier. After all, there could be hundreds of swimmers at any one time, many of whom would not have washed before entering and who would have walked to the poolside changing cubicles in their work clothes and shoes.

Accordingly, the price dropped, day by day, until finally, at the end of the cycle the entire pool was emptied, scrubbed down, and the whole process begun anew.

Not until the 1920s would showers and footbaths, or systems for circulating and filtering the water, as installed at the Victoria Baths, become commonplace.

Chlorination, the process which gives modern pools the distinctive smell swimmers know only too well, began around 1929-30.

Nor was the water as warm as

we are accustomed to nowadays, seldom rising above 22° Celsius (72° Fahrenheit), compared with today's norm of between 27-30°.

For this reason virtually all pre-war pools were boarded over during the coldest months and used as dance halls or gymnasiums. Some baths laid down matting for indoor bowls.

Strict segregation of the sexes was another norm. But more than that, the separate pools provided for women were always smaller than the men's. At Victoria Baths there were even two pools for men, First Class and Second Class.

The first Manchester baths to break with this distinction was Withington. In 1914, one year after it opened, parents were invited to swim together in the company of their children. So popular did this daring experiment prove that although Levenshulme Baths, opened on Barlow Road in 1921, still had twin pools, by the early 1930s, 13 of Manchester's 19 baths allowed mixed bathing.

Of all the public baths built in Manchester and Salford before 1914, only two remain in use: Withington (opened 1913) and Cromwell Road, Eccles (also 1913 but with 1927 additions), the latter for hydro-therapeutic use only.

Four baths from the inter-war period also still operate. In addition to Levenshulme, there are two neo-Georgian designs by the City's architects department under Henry Price. These are Chorlton Baths, Manchester Road (1929) and Broadway Baths, New Moston (1932). Worsley Pool, in Walkden, opened in 1937, also retains a number of interesting period details.

In the post war period new and larger competititon-sized pools were built at Sharston, in

1961 – an example of a new 'shop window' approach, allowing views inside the pool to attract more usage – and Broughton in 1967 (see pp126-127), before the 1970s saw water sports and dry sports brought under the same roof, at Wythenshawe Forum (1971), Moss Side (1974) and Miles Platting (1978). The age of the Leisure Centre had begun.

Allied to the contracting out of leisure management from the 1980s onwards, this trend developed further with the advent of a new breed of non-linear leisure pools, complete with flumes, sprays and wave machines.

The current trend is to upgrade existing pools by adding fitness centres and cafes, using the income to help maintain the pools. Even so, the total number of public pools in Manchester and Salford has halved since 1945, while private pools have proliferated in health clubs and hotels.

As this chapter has sought to show, the design and function of swimming pools is an ever evolving process, driven as much by public taste as by advances in building materials and water management systems.

But one thing is for sure; that as more historic baths fall out of use, finding a new role for them – like finding a use for so many of our redundant churches – presents a significant challenge for planners and conservationists alike.

For two of the nation's aquatic gems, the Victoria Baths and the Henry Square Baths in Ashton-under-Lyne, that process of finding a suitable adaptive re-use is already under way.

But for the crumbling Greengate Baths, where the story of modern baths began, at present, no life-belt is in sight.

▲ When the **Victoria Baths** opened on September 7 1906, resplendent in its Ruabon red-brick and terracotta trimmings, the *Manchester Guardian* reported: 'The building as a whole and its internal equipment and decoration make it probably the most splendid municipal bathing institution in the country.' Almost a century later that distinction still applies.

Even though the Grade II* baths closed in 1993 – despite a 16,000 signature petition and continuous lobbying by members of a specially formed trust – the baths is still held in awe and affection by the hundreds of visitors who take advantage of regular open days.

In 2002 English Heritage and the A6 Partnership funded £244,000 worth of emergency repairs in order to prevent further deterioration of the fabric. But two subsequent bids for Lottery funds to re-open the building as a Healthy Living Centre were rejected and the prospects looked bleak until, in 2003, the baths triumphed in BBC Television's *Restoration* series, attracting twice as many votes as its nearest rival and securing the promise of over £3 million worth of grant aid (ironically most of it from Lottery sources).

Studies are now in hand to see how best to proceed, given that it would cost £6 million to reopen the Turkish Bath, or up to £18-20 million to secure the whole structure and re-open one of the pools, as well as the Turkish Bath.

In short, the fight for this beautiful building is not over yet.

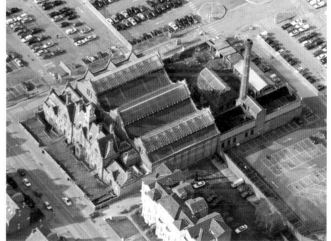

▶ This is the Males First Class Pool at the **Victoria Baths**, also known as the Gala Pool, with the City of Manchester's crest displayed proudly on the far end wall.

Here was an aquatic stadium for the city's swimming elite, a place where many a Mancunian watched swimming galas and water polo matches, and where in July 1912, the Hawaiian Olympic swimmer, Duke Kahanamoku, 'The Human Fish' – also known as the father of modern surfing – gave one of the first demonstrations in this country of the then unknown Australian stroke called front crawl. During the Second World War, local boys would dive in for sixpences thrown from the gallery by American GIs.

This was also the pool that in winter was boarded over and turned into a dance hall. A live orchestra played here right up until the 1950s.

Other facilities in the building included a Turkish Bath – much used by local businessmen as a place both to relax and to negotiate deals – and for the poorer classes, 64 slipper baths and a laundry, which in itself was a major focus of life for local housewives.

In 1952 the baths also installed the country's first public Aeratone, an early form of jacuzzi that apparently soothed many an injured footballer brought over from Maine Road and Old Trafford.

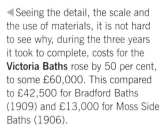

◀ Seeing the detail, the scale and the use of materials, it is not hard to see why, during the three years it took to complete, costs for the **Victoria Baths** rose by 50 per cent, to some £60,000. This compared to £42,500 for Bradford Baths (1909) and £13,000 for Moss Side Baths (1906).

Even so, it was the only baths to feature three pools, and was relatively good value compared, for example, with Haggerston Baths in east London, which opened in 1904 and had only one pool, and yet also cost around £60,000.

One expense which had not been envisaged was £4,788 spent on boring a deep underground well, in order to supply the pools with abundant supplies of fresh, clear water, rather than paying for the city's own, often tainted supply.

For extra durability all electrical wiring was routed through watertight pipes, and throughout the building ceramic tiles, Terrazzo and mosaic flooring were used for improved wear and tear and appearance. As the lead architect Henry Price argued before his detractors – and there were many – a building that would be hard-wearing, respected by its users, and yield lower maintenance costs, would, in the long term, be more cost effective for rate payers.

But not, alas, indefinitely. No baths designer can ever fully account for changing fashions, for the inevitable advances in technology that make baths like this one too expensive to maintain, or, just as importantly, for shifts in public policy.

Yet although the water palace has remained closed since 1993, its sheer quality shines on still.

Indeed, the Victoria Baths is one of those rare and precious buildings that virtually speaks for itself.

COPYRIGHT
URM. 77

URMSTON BATHS

LILYWHITE LTD.
BRIGHOUSE.

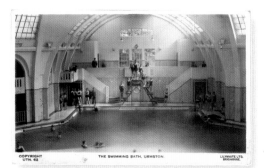

COPYRIGHT
UTN. 62

THE SWIMMING BATH, URMSTON

LILYWHITE LTD.
BRIGHOUSE.

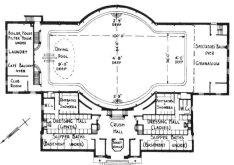

◄ Ever since Thomas Worthington's pioneering work in Manchester during the 1850s, designers of public baths have continually sought new forms, both to invoke civic pride and to attract new users.

Shown left is a prime example of this, the unique **Urmston Baths** in Trafford, built in 1933 for a mere £30,000 (half that of the Victoria Baths built 30 years earlier).

Notice how elegantly the pool, 100 feet in length, filled the space under the gracefully proportioned glazed dome (*centre left and right*), with two shallow areas for children in the curved wings. The design was by two Urmston District Council engineers, El Leeming and AN Potter (who also worked on the superb clubhouse for Davyhulme Park Golf Club in 1937 (*see p75*).

Urmston, unfortunately, was demolished in 1987 to make way for private houses

Sharston Baths (*shown below left in its model form*) on Brownley Road, Wythenshawe, was a competition-scale pool designed by one of Henry Price's successors as City Architect, Leonard C Howitt. This was even shorter-lived, being open only from 1961 until 1989.

Sharston demonstrated how pool design was moving away from top-lit, glazed roofing – often problematic – towards large span, solid roofs with glazed curtain walls.

▲ **Broughton Pool** (*top left and right*), Great Cheetham Street West, was Salford City Council's first post-war pool development. Costing £380,000 and opened in 1967, it was designed by Scott Brownrigg & Turner, in association with LG Mouchel & Partners. Now looking smarter than ever following a revamp funded by a Single Regeneration Budget grant, Broughton represents a further stage in 20th century pool design.

With nearly 400 seats in its spectator gallery the pool is now a favourite for staging local and regional galas, a role Sharston used to fulfil in south Manchester. Not visible here are the pyramid-shaped skylights set in the roof, which add interest to its exterior profile.

Broughton's distinct linear and horizontal emphases contrast with the more curvaceous profile of the **Manchester Aquatics Centre**, Oxford Road (*above and above right*). Designed by the leisure specialists FaulknerBrowns (who also worked extensively at Sportcity, *see Chapter Five*), in conjunction with Arup Consulting Engineers, the £32.2 million centre opened in September 2000 and was initially geared towards hosting the 2002 Commonwealth Games. As Britain's only venue with two 50m pools, one of which is located in the basement, the Aquatics Centre offers vital training facilities for the nation's top swimmers, but is also used by local aqua sports clubs and by the general public. A series of moveable floors and booms allow the main pool to be reconfigured to varying depths and sizes for different events, while at one end a flume and some palm trees add a popular touch for leisure users.

Chapter Eighteen

Conclusions

The example of the Moor Lane sports ground, Salford (*see p37*) illustrates the lack of specific protection currently in place for historic sports grounds. Its 1930s stand (*above*) is unlikely to be listed, yet the ground itself is clearly an historic landscape, having been in continuous use for sport since at least the 1680s. Moor Lane already enjoys a measure of protection under Salford's UDP and under government guidance relating to open spaces, sport and recreation (PPG 17). But it would also benefit from the added protection afforded by its inclusion on English Heritage's Register of Historic Parks and Gardens. Several other sporting sites around Britain fall into a similar category.

As one newspaper commented after the closing ceremony of the Commonwealth Games in 2002, 'Give Manchester a medal!'

We can imagine no better place to have started our investigations into Britain's sporting heritage. Certainly English Heritage has been impressed by the sheer range and quality of the sports related buildings and sites to have emerged from this groundbreaking study. Even local experts have expressed surprise.

But our *Played in Manchester* report is not an end in itself.

This study has raised a number of issues, some of which relate specifically to Manchester's sporting heritage, whilst others are of more general relevance to the nation's sporting past.

Many of these issues are too complex to be summed up adequately in a few sentences. Nevertheless it is hoped that the brief points which follow will draw attention to the nature and range of issues affecting our sporting heritage and, in doing so, will assist all interested parties in tackling them.

Historic sports buildings

In common with all buildings and structures of historic or architectural significance, buildings for sport are already eligible for protection under the current system of listing.

Indeed several listed buildings are featured within this book.

There are, however, a number of unlisted buildings which, as a result of this study, may merit consideration. Candidates might include the Old Trafford Bowling Club (*see p83*), the former Manchester Grammar School pavilion (*pp1 and 43*), and the clubhouse at Davyhulme Golf Club (*p75*). It will be interesting to see if readers feel strongly about other featured buildings.

Sports clubs have ever changing needs and listing is perceived by some as hampering both day-to-day management and long-term planning, whilst adding to overall costs. Any further listing of sports buildings would therefore need to be taken forward in collaboration with those managing and using sports facilities, and be supported by wider information and support.

Historic sports grounds

At present, all sports grounds and open spaces enjoy a measure of protection under the government's Planning Policy Guidance Note 17, and at a local level, under Unitary Development Plans. Some grounds also fall within conservation areas.

However, unlike historic buildings, there are as yet no specific mechanisms in place to provide added protection to sports grounds of particular historic significance (of which, in Manchester, Moor Lane would certainly be one, *see left*).

One possible solution would be for these grounds to be included on the Register of Historic Parks and Gardens, which is maintained by English Heritage.

This would ensure that their historic merit is taken into consideration should a change of use be sought through the planning system.

Given that a major review of heritage designation has been under way since November 2002, now would seem an opportune time to consider this possibility.

Buildings at Risk

It is clear that a number of historic sports buildings have fallen out of use and their future is in doubt. In recent years, for example, much attention has focused on the plight of the Victoria Baths, Hathersage Road. And rightly so. It is a building of national importance.

However, the fate of two other buildings in the Manchester area – both historically and architecturally significant – should also be a cause of great concern.

These are the now derelict Greengate Baths, on Collier Street, Salford (pp116-117) – which unfortunately has defied adaptive re-use for some years – and the Manchester Ice Palace, Derby Street (pp97-99), the oldest ice rink in Britain, now lying vacant.

Maintaining historic buildings

There appears to be no shortage of advice available to sports clubs wishing to build new facilities, either from Sport England or from specialist architects, consultants and planners in the sports and leisure industry.

Clubs that own historic properties are less well served. There is, as a result, a desperate need for specific guidance to be made available, together with other forms of support.

We found many voluntary club workers struggling to maintain buildings and grounds which form an integral part of the local scene, and often provide important social outreach for elderly and disadvantaged members of the community.

For them, the notion of conservation comes a poor second to survival. If inappropriate roof tiles or window frames are all that can be afforded, then difficult choices have to be made.

Sporting bodies must share with organisations such as English Heritage, the Heritage Lottery Fund and local authorities, some of the responsibility for maintaining and enhancing our historic environment and provide guidance and incentives for those clubs that act as unpaid guardians of our sporting heritage.

Education and outreach

Educational initiatives – such as one run in 2002 by English Heritage in conjunction with Plymouth Grove School on the Victoria Baths in 2002 (*see Links*) – suggest that there is considerable scope for using sporting heritage to support a wide range of teaching subjects.

Schoolchildren and students can learn a great deal about their locality and about history in the wider context through the medium of sport. As this study shows, Manchester offers plenty of rich source material.

Local history and tourism

Much of what we have learnt of sporting heritage in the Manchester area has come to us via local historians.

Their knowledge, plus the added evidence gathered by our study, offers a number of opportunities to enhance the city's attractiveness to visitors and tourists.

Sports heritage trails in Trafford Park and the Irwell Valley could be of particular interest, for example, along the lines of other trails already in place.

Commemorative plaques

Manchester City Council, among other local authorities in the area, already has an established programme of commemorative

plaques, three of which are illustrated in this book (*see pp17, 52 and 114*).

Our study clearly indicated that a national programme of plaques relating to sporting heritage would be welcomed. Green was the favoured colour.

Another suggestion was that a Sports Heritage Trust be set up to administer the scheme and provide wider support.

Locations in Manchester that might be considered include the former Botanical Gardens gateway (pp21 and 27), and the sites of the Fallowfield Stadium (p62), James Rawson's grave (p79), and the Rusholme Glacarium (pp94-96).

There may also be a case for a plaque at the Belle Vue Greyhound Stadium, perhaps mounted on the former turnstile block (p69), which itself offers an excellent opportunity for a public memorial to the Belle Vue area as a whole, and also to the stadium's status as Britain's first greyhound track.

Future studies

Played in Britain will now turn its attention to other cities and other specific areas of sporting heritage. For details, see Links.

The Manchester City Experience – Manchester City's much praised club museum at the City of Manchester Stadium, Sportcity – has proved immensely popular since its inauguration in April 2004. Club museums, or museums concentrating on a single sport, such as the Lawn Tennis Museum at Wimbledon, clearly appeal to a targeted audience. Is there scope for another sports-related museum in Manchester?

Links

Abbreviations
MUP: Manchester University Press
TLACS: Transactions of the Lancashire
and Cheshire Antiquarian Society

Where no publisher listed assume
self-published by club or author

Where no date listed assume
published on final date within
title, ie. 1860-1960 means published
1960

Sports history general
Birley D *Sport and the Making of Britain* MUP (1993)
Birley D *Land of Sport and Glory: Sport and British
    Society 1887-1910* MUP (1995)
Birley D *Playing the Game: Sport and British Society
    1910-1945* MUP (1995)
Brailsford D *British Sport: A Social History* Lutterworth (1997)
Cox RW, Jarvie G and Vamplew W
    Encyclopedia of British Sport ABC-CLIO (2000)
Dobbs B *Edwardians at Play: 1890-1914* Pelham (1973)
Henricks TS *Disputed Pleasures: Sport and Society in
    Pre-industrial England* Greenwood Press (1991)
Hill J *Sport, Leisure and Culture in Twentieth Century Britain*
    Palgrave (2002)
Holt R *Sport and the British: A Modern History* OUP (1989)
Holt R ed. *Sport and the Working Class* Clarendon (1990)
Lowerson J *Sport and the English Middle Classes 1870-1914*
    MUP (1993)
Reeves AC *Pleasures and Pastimes in Medieval England*
    OUP (1998)
Strutt J *The Sports and Pastimes of the People of England*
    Firecrest Publishing (1801, reprinted 1969)
Walton JK and Walvin J eds. *Leisure in Britain 1780-1939*
    MUP (1986)
Walvin J *Leisure and Society 1830-1950* Longman (1978)
www2.umist.ac.uk/sport/index2.html
    British Society of Sports Historians (based at UMIST)

Reports
English Heritage *Power of Place: The Future of the
    Historic Environment* (2002)
DCMS *The Historic Environment: A Force for our Future*
    (2001)
DTLR *Improving Urban Parks, Play Areas and Open Spaces*
    (2002)
Local Government Association *The Value of Parks
    and Open Spaces* (2001)
Sport England/CABE *Better Places for Sport* (2003)
www.english-heritage.org.uk
www.culture.gov.uk
www.odpm.gov.uk
www.cabe.org
www.savebritainsheritage.org
www.sportengland.org

Manchester general
Archer JHG *Art and Architecture in Victorian Manchester*
    MUP (1985)
Bergin T, Pearce DN and Shaw S eds. *Salford: A City and
    its Past* Salford Cultural Services (1989)
Cooper G *The Illustrated History of Manchester's Suburbs*
    Breedon (2002)
Earwaker JP ed. *Court Leet Records of the Manor of
    Manchester* (1884)
Farrer W and Brownbill J *Victoria County History of
    Lancashire* (1907-14)
Greenall RL *The Making of Victorian Salford* Carnegie (2002)
Hartwell C *Manchester* Pevsner Architectural Guides (2001)
Kidd A *Manchester* Edinburgh University Press (2002)
Manchester Corporation *How Manchester is Managed* (1927)
Manchester Corporation *City of Manchester Plan* (1945)
www.manchester.gov.uk
www.manchester2002-uk.com
www.salford.gov.uk
www.tameside.gov.uk
www.stockport.gov.uk
www.trafford.gov.uk
www.manchestercivic.org.uk

Chapter 1. Played in Manchester
Allaby D *Wimbledon of the North: 100 years at the Northern*
    EJ Mortern (1981)
Bancroft JW *Olympic Champions in Manchester*
    High Aim Productions (1993)
Fallowfield Bowling & Lawn Tennis Club *Centenary
    Brochure 1860-1960*
Jones SG *Working Class Sport in Manchester between
    the Wars* in *Sport and the Working Class*
    MUP (1990)
Scott D and Bent C *Borrowed Time: A Social History of
    Running. Salford Harriers, 1884-1984*
Morris G *Rugby League in Manchester* Tempus (2003)
Ruff A *The Biography of Philips Park 1846-1996* (2000)
Taubman A, Webb P and Wetton J *Everyone's a Winner:
    The history of sport in and around Manchester*
    Manchester Museum of Science and
    Technology (1990)
Wilson W *Sale Harriers - 75 Years of Athletics* (1986)
www.mcrh.mmu.ac.uk Manchester Centre for Regional History

Chapter 2. Trafford Park

Bellers L *The Unseen Archives, A Photographic History of Manchester United* Mustard (1999)

Green G *There's Only One United – the Centenary History of Manchester United* Coronet (1979)

Hayhurst K *The Pictorial History of Lancashire County Cricket Club* Polar (2000)

Kelly S *The Old Trafford Encyclopedia* Mainstream (1998)

Lorimer M and Ambrose D *Cricket Grounds of Lancashire* Association of Cricket Statisticians (1992)

McCartney I *Old Trafford - Theatre of Dreams* Yore (1996)

Manchester Polo Club *Handbook* (1920)

Marshall J *Old Trafford* Pelham (1971)

Nicholls R *Trafford Park: The First 100 Years* Phillimore (1996)

Powell W. A *The Wisden Guide to Cricket Grounds* (1992)

Roberts J *The Team that Wouldn't Die: the Story of the Busby Babes* Methuen (1998)

Tyrrell T *The Illustrated History of Manchester United 1878-1999* Hamlyn (1999)

Urmston UDC *Urmston 41 Years On, 1933-74*

Wynne-Thomas P *The History of Lancashire County Cricket Club* Chrisopher Helm (1989)

www.lccc.co.uk Lancashire CCC Museum

www.manutd.com Manchester United Museum

http://manchesterhistory.net/whitecity.html White City

Chapter 3. Irwell Valley

Axon E *Early Manchester Horse Races* TLACS (May 1913)

Corbett J *River Irwell: Pleasant Reminiscences of the 19th Century and Suggestions for Improvements in the 20th* (1907)

Dobkin M *Broughton & Cheetham Hill in Regency and Victorian Times* Neil Richardson

Logan W A *The Agecroft Story: The First Hundred years of the Agecroft Rowing Club, 1861-1960* Agecroft Trustees (1960)

Lorimer M and Ambrose D *Cricket Grounds of Lancashire* Association of Cricket Statisticians (1992)

Ramsden C *Farewell Manchester: A History of Manchester Racecourse* Allen (1966)

Thompson P *On the Turf: the origins of horse racing in the north west* Quarry Publications (1991)

www.irwellsculpturetrail.co.uk

www.manchesterjewishmuseum.com

Chapter 4. Belle Vue

Bamford R, Jarvis J *Homes of British Speedway* Tempus (2001)

Fleming D *The Manchester Fighters* Neil Richardson (1986)

Genders R *NGRC Book of Greyhound Racing* Pelham (1990)

Greyhound Racing Association *Belle Vue Greyhound Racecourse 50th Anniversary* (1976)

Hughes B *Jackie Brown: the Man, the Myth, the Legend* Manchester Free Press (1995)

Hughes B *Jock McAvoy: Portrait of a Fighting Legend* Empire (2002)

Hughes B *Johnny King: King and Country* Manchester Free Press (1995)

Herbert M *Never Counted Out: the story of Len Johnson* Dropped Aitches Press (1992)

MEN *The Aces Golden Years 1928-78* (1978)

Nicholls R *The Belle Vue Story* Neil Richardson (1983)

Rogers M *The Illustrated History of Speedway* Studio Publication (1978)

www.geocities.com/Athens/Atrium/4182/BelleVue.html

http://manchesterhistory.net/BelleVue.html

www.chethams.org.uk

Chapter 5. Sportcity

www.arup.com

www.eis2win.co.uk English Institute of Sport

www.faulknerbrowns.co.uk

www.gameslegacy.com 2002 Commonwealth Games

www.manchestervelodrome.com National Cycling Centre

www.mcfc.co.uk Manchester City Experience

www.neweastmanchester.co.uk

Chapter 6. Stadiums and Grounds

Barak M *A Century of Rugby at Sale* (1962)

Barlow TM, Fletcher JR *A History of the Manchester Wheelers Club 1883-1983* viewable at *www.wheelers.org*

Bayley N *The Kippax, A Celebration* Electric Blue (1994)

Delaney T *The Grounds of Rugby League* (1991)

Gatenby P *Standing Ovation: A Tribute to the Kippax* (1994)

Hillsborough Stadium Disaster 15 April 1989: Inquiry by the Rt Hon Lord Justice Taylor, Final Report The Stationery Office, Cmd 962 (1990)

Inglis S *The Football Grounds of Britain* Collins Willow (1996)

Inglis S *Sightlines: A Stadium Odyssey* Yellow Jersey (2000)

James G *Farewell to Maine Road* Polar (2003)

Chapter 6. Stadiums and Grounds cont.

James G *Manchester, The Greatest City* Polar (1997)
Morris G *Images of Sport: Salford Rugby League Club*
    Tempus (2000)
Platt D *A History of Salford Rugby League Club* (1991)
Richards W *Manchester Athletics Club: The First 100 years*
    1886-1986
Sale RFC *Sale Rugby Football Club: 125 years 1861-1986*
Salford Reporter *Salford Rugby League Football Club,*
    100 Years of Rugby League 1879-1979
Swinton RLFC *A History of the Club, 1867-1929*

Chapter 7. Turnstiles

www.broughton-controls.co.uk
www.gunneboentrance.com

Chapter 8. Clubs and Pavilions

Balaam L *Manchester Football Club, 1860-1985*
Bentley J *Dare to be Wise - A History of Manchester Grammar*
    School James & James (1990)
English Heritage *Golf Course Proposals in Historic*
    Landscapes: an English Heritage statement (1991)
Fiddes E *History of Owens College and of Manchester*
    University 1853-1914 (1937)
Peers MW *A History of the Manchester Golf Club 1882-1982*
Rice J *The Pavilion Book of Pavilions* Pavilion Books (1991)
Russell JM *Old Manchester Golf Club 1818-1988*
Worsley Golf Club *The History of Worsley Golf Club*
    1894-1994

Chapter 9. Archery

Axon WEA *Archery in Manchester in the 16th and 17th*
    Centuries TLACS Vol 18 (1900)
Credland AG *Journal of the Society of Archer-Antiquaries*
    various articles (1989 ff)
Roberts T *English Bowmen* EP Publishing (1801)
Smith WJ *Sir Ashton Lever of Alkington* TLACS Vol 72 (1965)
museum.man.ac.uk/collections/archery/archery.htm
    Simon Collection at Manchester Museum
www.bio.vu.nl/thb/users/kooi/saaflder.html
    Society of Archer-Antiquaries
www.eac-online.co.uk Eccles Archery Club
www.asshetonbowmen.com
www.gnas.org Grand National Archery Society

Chapter 10. Bowls

Ayers ET *Bowls, Bowling Greens, Bowl Playing* Jarrold (1894)
Evans RDC *Bowling Greens: their history, construction*
    and maintenance STRI (1992)
Sudell R and Tennyson Waters D *Sports Buildings and*
    Playing Fields Batsford (1957)
www.bowls.org British Crown Green Bowling Association
www.bowlsengland.com English Bowling Assocaition
www.premierbowls.co.uk

Chapter 11. Real tennis

Aberdare Lord *The JT Faber Book of Tennis and Rackets*
    Quiller Press (2001)
Gillmeister H *Tennis: A Cultural History*
    Leicester University Press (1997)
Kenyon N *The Manchester Tennis and Racquet Club*
    1876-1980
www.mtrc.co.uk
www.realtennis.gbrit.com

Chapter 12. Lacrosse

Beers WG *Report on the 1883 Tour* Boy's Own Paper (1883)
Malkin T *The Oldest Lacrosse Club* Stockport Lacrosse
    Club (1996)
Melland N *How to Play Lacrosse* (1909)
www.englishlacrosse.co.uk
www.hattersleys.com
www.stockportlacrosse.co.uk

Chapter 13. Skating

Crainer S *The Manchester Ice Palace and a Short History of*
    Lancashire Dairies Lancashire Dairies (1985)
Crawford G *Cultural Tourists and Cultural Trends;*
    Commercialisation and the Coming of the Storm
    Culture Sport, Society, Frank Cass (Spring 2002)
Drackett P *Flashing Blades: The Story of British Ice Hockey*
    Crowood (1987)
Drake Digby J *Skating and Curling* Phipps and Connor (1893)
Manchester Ice Palace *Silver Jubilee Programme* (1936)
Pout R *The Early Years of English Roller Hockey*
    1885-1914 (1993)
Smith A *The Puck Chasers of Manchester* TLH
www.azhockey.com
www.iceskate-magazine.com

Chapter 14. Lads' Clubs

Eager W McG *Making Men, a History of Boys' Clubs* University of London (1953)

Flint R *Openshaw Lads' Club Diamond Jubilee Report* (1948)

Gatenby P *Morrissey's Manchester* Empire (2002)

Hill H *The Story of the Adelphi Lads Club, 1888-1948*

Russell CEB *Manchester Boys, Sketches of Manchester Lads at Work and Play* (1905)

Salford Lads' Club *Annual Report 1908*

Schill PH *History of the Ardwick Lads' and Mens' Club* (1935)

Whitbourn F *'Lex' the biography of Alexander Devine* Longmans, Green (1937)

www.gmfcyp.org.uk Greater Manchester Federation of Clubs for Young People

www.nacyp.org.uk National Association of CYPP

www.newbarracks.org.uk

www.salfordladsclub.org.uk

Chapter 15. Billiards

Clare N *Billiards and Snooker Bygones* Shire (1996)

Sigsworth Eric M *Montague Burton, The Tailor of Taste* MUP (1990)

www.eaba.co.uk English Amateur Billiards Association

www.tradgames.org.uk

Chapter 16. Air racing

Maher P ed. *The Lancashire Aero Club 1922-1992* LAC (1992)

www.bartonaerodrome.co.uk

www.lancsaeroclub.co.uk

www.thosemagnificentmen.co.uk/manchester

Chapter 17. Swimming

Pass AJ *Thomas Worthington: Victorian Architecture and Social Purpose* Manchester Literary & Philosophical Society (1988)

Pettigrew WW *Municipal Parks: Layout, Management and Administration* Journal of Park Administration VMH (1937)

SAVE *Taking the Plunge – The Architecture of Bathing* (1982)

Select Committee on Culture, Media and Sport *Testing the Waters: The Sport of Swimming* (2002)

Williams P *Victoria Baths: Manchester's Water Palace* Spire (2004)

www.victoriabaths.org.uk

www.victorianturkishbath.org

www.londonpoolscampaign.com

Chapter 18. Conclusions

DCMS *Protecting our Historic Environment: making the system better* (2003) downloadable from *www.culture.gov.uk*

English Heritage Schools Education Programme *Getting in the Swim: Exploring Manchester's Water Palace* video (2002) available from *www.english-heritage.org.uk/education*

ODPM *Planning Policy Guidance 17: Planning for open space, sport and recreation* (2002) downloadable from *www.odpm.gov.uk*

www.english-heritage.org.uk Register of Historic Parks and Gardens Register of Buidings at Risk

www.manchester.gov.uk/planning/heritage/plaques.htm

Further titles already in preparation as part of the *Played in Britain* series are:

Engineering Archie – Archibald Leitch, football ground designer

Liquid Assets – the best of British lidos

Bowled Over – the bowling greens of Britain

Great Lengths – the best of British swimming pools

Top Tables – British billiards and snooker – the look, the lifestyle

Plus:

Played in Birmingham, Played in Liverpool and *Played in Glasgow*

For details and a chance to add your comments and suggestions, see *www.playedinbritain.co.uk*

Credits

Photographs and images

Please note that in the credits below, where more than one photograph appears on a page, each photograph is identified by a letter, starting with 'a' in the top left hand corner of the page, or at the top, and continuing thereafter in a *clockwise* direction.

English Heritage/National Monuments Record photographs

Nigel Corrie: 32b, 38b, 39b, 41a, 41b, 41c, 41d, 72b, 72c, 73a, 77a, 80, 82b, 91, 104a, 105, 108a, 108b, 109a, 109b, 110, 111a, 111b, 112a, 112c, 114a, 119a, 119b, 127b; Bob Skingle: cover flap, back cover b, 27c, 40b, 50b, 55a, 55c, 74, 82a, 84a, 84b, 89a, 89b, 89c, 89d, 92, 93b, 93c, 106, 117b, 117c, 120a, 120b, 123a, 127c, 127d, 136; Damian Grady: 29, 38a, 60a, 61a, 61b, 71a, 71b, 87b, 101b, 115a, 123b; Paul McDonald: 124, 125f; National Monuments Record: 119c

Commissioned photographs

Simon Inglis: back cover c and d, 1, 6a, 6d, 7, 9, 10, 11, 14a, 16a, 16b, 16d, 19, 21a, 30b, 31, 32a, 32c, 34, 37, 43c, 52, 53, 66a, 79b, 81b, 82c, 83a, 83b, 84c, 97a, 99a, 102, 104b, 112b, 115b, 122b, 128; David Brearley: back cover a, 4, 6c, 17b, 60b, 75, 85, 87a, 88a, 122a; Ed Garvey: 47b, 51, 55b, 57a, 57b, 58, 129; Mark Leach: 76, 78b; Mark Watson: 64, 125a, 125b, 125d, 125e, 125g; New East Manchester: 54

Archive photographs

Manchester Central Library Local Studies Unit: cover, 15b, 18b, 27b, 36a, 36b, 39a, 42a, 48-49, 62, 68, 69, 73b, 81a, 84d, 96a, 96b, 98c, 113, 114b, 126c;

Salford Museum and Art Gallery, Local History Library: inside cover, 42b, 42c, 43a, 43b; Chetham's Library: 14b, 15a, 21b, 22, 44, 45; Manchester Art Gallery/Platt Hall Museum of Costume: 18a, 95a; Derek Adrian and Jean Zwiggelaar Adrian: 20b, 46-47; Manchester Airviews: 2, 28; Arup Sport: 56, 61c; John Dawson/cricketimages.co.uk: 30a; John Fryer/www.fryer-foto.com: 90; Bernard Gallagher: 66b; Don Gardner, Royal Toxophilite Society: 78a, 79a; Getty Images: 33, 50a; House of Images: 26a, 27a; Illustrated London News: 24; Don Johnson, Trafford Sport Development: 63a; Lancashire CCC Museum: 8; Bill McLaughlin: 59a; Manchester Evening News Syndication: 40a, 100c; manchesterimages.com: 101a; Manchester Museum: 78c; Manchester United Museum: 6b, 65a; Joe Martin, Conservation Officer, Salford City Council: 135; David Montford: 125c; Oldham Chronicle: 77b; picturesofmanchester.com: 127a; Simmons Aerofilms: 20A; Stephen Wild: 59b; Stephen Wright/www.smithsphotos.com: 107a; John Holmes, Trafford Parks and Countryside Service: 63b; Trafford Local Studies: 25, 26b; The Wellcome Trust: 118

Donated photographs

English Heritage wish to thank the following individuals and organisations for providing photographs and source material: Len Balaam: 70; Dr Ian Gordon/Leach Colour Ltd: 126a, 126d; Gwen Fitton: 65b; Gunnebo: 66c; TS Hattersley's: 93a; Jeremy Kearns: 94, 97b, 98a, 98b, 98c, 98e, 99b, 100a, 100b; Arthur Little: 117a; Ted Pearson: 67a, 67b; Salford Lads' Club: 103, 107b; Tom Sharp: 72a; Joan Slater: inside back cover, 98d; Robert Stevenson: 16c, 46; Tennis and Rackets Association: 88b; Victoria Baths Trust: 116

Journals and publications

Architect and Building News; Architects Journal; Athletic News; Bowlers World; British Architect and Northern Engineer; British Journal of Sports History; Building Design; Cheshire Historian; Cheshire Life; Conservation Bulletin; Country Life; Groundtastic; Illustrated London News; Illustrated Sporting and Dramatic News; Lancashire Life; Manchester City News; Manchester Courier; Manchester Evening Chronicle; Manchester Evening News; Manchester Gazette; Manchester Guardian; Manchester Region History Review; Manchester Weekly Times; South Manchester Gazette; Sporting and Dramatic News; The Sphinx; The Looking Glass

Acknowledgements

The author would like to thank all those many individuals, organisations and club representatives who assisted with both the original English Heritage study, *A Sporting Chance*, and the subsequent production of *Played in Manchester*. In particular, Malcolm Cooper has been a stalwart supporter of the project from its earliest days, as as has Martin Cherry at Savile Row, and all the team at English Heritage publications in Swindon; Val Horsler, Rob Richardson, Robin Taylor and René Rodgers. Further thanks are due to Henry Owen-John, Lindsay Moutrey and Laura Dobson (NW Region), Steve Coles and Tony Cannadine (Cambridge), Elain Harwood and Mark Fenton (London) and Jane Lawrence of Direct PR.

It should also be acknowledged that this project would not have taken place without the commitment and energy of Jason Wood, of Heritage Consultancy Services. Manchester City Council and in particular Peter Babb, Head of Planning, have also been of great help.

On a more personal note, the author would also like to thank Clare Hartwell for her expertise and companionship throughout this study, Terry Wyke for his invaluable comments on the text, Jackie Spreckley of Malavan Media for additional research and support, the Saffer family for logistical support and Doug Cheeseman for making this book look so fine.

The Manchester area is well blessed with excellent archives and even more excellent archivists and librarians. For their knowledge, enthusiasm and amazing patience, profuse thanks are due to Paula Moorhouse, Richard Bond and George Turnbull at Manchester Central Library's Local Studies Unit; Tim Ashworth at the Salford Local History Library; Sheila O'Hare and Jan Shearsmith at Trafford Local Studies; Fergus Wilde and Michael Powell at Chetham's Library; Marion Hewitt of the North West Film Archive at Manchester Metropolitan University, and Wendy Hodkinson of the Simon Archery Collection at Manchester Museum.

Thanks also to Architects Britch, Atherden Fuller Leng, Peter Ainsworth, Roy Armson, Dennis Bird (National Ice Skating Association), Sue Brooks (Crossley House), Steve Burrows (Arup Associates), Joan Campbell, John Collier (Old Trafford Bowling Club), Margaret Conroy, Les Cotton, Garry Crawford, John Crowther (British Crown Green Bowling Association), Norman Ellison, Sasha Essuah-Mensah (Trafford Community Parks Officer), Tony Fare (Worsley Cricket Club), John Gilburn and Liz Murphy (Belle Vue Greyhound Stadium), Leslie Grainger (Stockport Lacrosse Club), Bob Hallows (Denton Cricket Club), Albert Harris (Crossley House), Keith Hayhurst (Lancashire CCC), Tony Henshaw (Worsley Golf Club), Leslie Holmes (Salford Lads' Club), Hugh Hornby (National Football Museum), Brian Hughes, Peter Hunter (National Association of Clubs for Young People), Dr Ian Gordon, Gary James (The Manchester City Experience), Emma Johns (British Greyhound Racing Board), Jeremy Kearns (Lancashire Dairies), Jim Kelly (Greater Manchester Federation of Clubs for Young People), Dave Lennard (Grange Club), Jackie McGuinness, Sean McHale (Ardwick Lads' Club), Joe Martin (Salford City Council), Graham Morris, Diana Naden (Commissions in the Environment), Geoff Ogden (Ellesmere Sports Club), Dame Kathleen Ollerenshaw, Anthony Pass, Diana Phillips; Simon Ramsden, Tom Sharp (Davyhulme Golf Club), Dave Swanton (Sale Sharks), David Tarry (Salford Reds), Adam Thomas, Jack Turner, Linda Walkden (CWS), Bill Williams (Manchester Jewish Museum), Gill Wright (Victoria Baths Trust), Harry Wright (Stockport Lads' Club) and Mark Wylie (Manchester United Museum).

Kersal Moor was last used for horse racing in 1847, but recent investigations by Salford conservation officers have discovered the embedded remains of what is thought to be the base of a marshall's box by the side of the former course.

Following page Boarded up but not forgotten, the Victoria Baths in Hathersage Road, where the battle to secure the building's future continues. Both cases show how much more needs to be done to safeguard sporting heritage in the Manchester area.